Ready to Lead with AI

A Practical Guide for School Leaders

Kip Glazer

ConnectEDD Publishing
Hanover, Pennsylvania

Th i s publication is available at discount pricing when purchased in quantity for educational purposes, promotions, or fundraisers. For inquiries and details, contact the publisher at: info@connecteddpublishing.com

Published by ConnectEDD Publishing LLC
Hanover, PA
www.connecteddpublishing.com

Cover Design: Kheila Casas

Ready to Lead with AI —1st ed. Paperback
ISBN   979-8-9933701-0-1

Ready to Lead with AI

Praise for *Ready to Lead with AI*

I strongly recommend this book as a must read for any administrator leading schools and systems in the age of AI. It speaks directly to the real pressures and responsibilities we carry, not in abstract terms, but through the lens of human-centered leadership. What makes this book powerful is how it validates the tension administrators feel between urgency and intentionality while offering guidance that keeps values, trust, and people at the center of decision making. This book challenges leaders to strengthen relationships across the entire system, from district offices and teaching staff to extended staff, students, families, and the broader field. I appreciate how the book elevates student voice, family transparency, and inclusive leadership as non-negotiables rather than add-ons. Most importantly, this book serves as a reminder that effective leadership in an AI-driven world is not about chasing the latest tools, but about clarity, courage, and staying grounded in our humanity. I would encourage any administrator looking to lead with purpose, integrity, and long-term impact to read this book and reflect on how their leadership choices shape the future of learning.

–Rudy Escobar | STEM & Computer Science Coordinator at
Stanislaus County Office of Ed and CSforCA Co-Chair

This book provides tried and tested strategies by Principal Dr. Kip Glazer, leading at the cutting edge of AI implementation at a public high school in Silicon Valley. She shares her story, key lessons, and steps to help principals on their journey to developing and refining AI policies and practices at school in collaboration with the district office, teachers, staff, students, families, and the field. This is the go-to-guide that school leaders need to innovate and transform so that youth voice and agency are centered in preparing for the future of AI.

–Dr. Jennifer Elemen | Digital Mediated Learning Coordinator
at US Berkeley School of Education and Past President of
California Council for the Social Studies.

Kip Glazer has written the book every school leader needs right now—not a theoretical treatise on AI, but a practitioner's guide grounded in the daily reality of leading schools. Having spent my career as an education leader, including as a high school principal, I know how rare it is to find a colleague who translates cutting-edge developments into actionable strategies while keeping students and educators at the center. I'm especially grateful that Kip focuses on teaching and learning first, positioning technology as support for what our learners need. Her journey from reluctant principal to thoughtful AI advocate mirrors the path many of us must take—stepping into the arena not because we have all the answers, but because our communities deserve courageous, humble leadership. This book offers honest stories, practical frameworks, and hard-won wisdom from real decisions with real consequences.

–Jean-Claude Brizard | President and CEO, Digital Promise Global & Former School Superintendent

Ready to Lead with AI is a timely and necessary guide for school leaders navigating one of the most consequential shifts in education. Kip Glazer keeps teaching and learning at the center while offering a clear, practical roadmap for engaging educators, students, families, and systems with transparency and trust. What I appreciate most is the balance: urgency and innovation, paired with the humility and humanity this moment demands. If you lead a school or system and want to navigate AI with clarity, confidence, and care, this book is an essential place to begin.

–Tiffany C. Taylor | President, ASU+GSV Summit

Dr. Kip Glazer brings knowledge and real-world know-how to create powerful stories and guidance. Her experiences with research projects make her researcher-practitioner collaboration chapter a blueprint we've been waiting for. School leaders, if you're interested in research, we're excited to meet you. Researchers, Chapter 7 gives important perspective for partnerships and should be required reading.

–Judi Fusco, Ph.D. | Director of Emerging Technologies and
Learning Sciences, Digital Promise

Ready to Lead with AI keeps pedagogy and purpose at the center of AI leadership. Kip Glazer offers school leaders practical, ethically-grounded guidance for integrating AI in ways that strengthen teaching and learning while engaging educators, students, families, and communities in responsible, inclusive decision-making.

–Katherine Goyette | Computer Science Coordinator for California
Department of Education; Co-author of *The Complete EdTech
Coach* and *History Matters in an Age of AI*

Ready to Lead with AI is exactly what school leaders need right now: clear, grounded, and deeply human. Kip Glazer brings rare credibility as a practicing principal with research and policy background, who understands both the promise and the pressure of leading in an AI age. This is a practical, trustworthy guide for education leaders who want to move forward with confidence, care, and purpose.

–Isabelle C. Hau | Executive Director, Stanford Accelerator for
Learning; Author of *Love to Learn*

Dr. Kip Glazer's *Ready to Lead with AI* is a bold, practical, and deeply inspiring extension of this vision in the age of artificial intelligence. Drawing from her real-world experience as a high school principal in Silicon Valley, Kip shows school leaders how to move beyond viewing AI as a mere tool or threat. Instead, she demonstrates how to harness it as a catalyst for authentic student agency, turning students from passive recipients into active co-creators, national presenters, policy innovators, and ethical AI leaders.

What sets this book apart is its unwavering commitment to the heart of learner agency: building trusting structures, gradually releasing responsibility, learning alongside students, and setting ambitious yet achievable goals that ripple outward. Kip's stories—from student-led AI webinars viewed by thousands to collaborative tools like the AI Policy Pathway—illustrate how AI, when guided by principled leadership, amplifies student voice and ownership in ways we could only dream of before.

For any principal or school leader seeking to foster environments where students "take flight" today—not just prepare for tomorrow—this book is an essential guide. It reminds us that true innovation begins when we get out of the way and let learners lead. Highly recommended—Kip Glazer doesn't just write about leading with AI; she lives it, and her results speak volumes.

–Jeanette Westfall | Co-author, *Learner Agency: A Field Guide for Taking Flight*, Educator and Advocate for Student-Centered Learning

Kip Glazer knows how to get things done--and she's ready to share. In *Ready to Lead with AI: A Practical Guide for School Leaders*, she tells marvelously candid and relatable stories about how, as a school principal, she is thoughtfully leading her community of teachers, students, staff and family through the complexities of AI. Her seasoned advice will become many other school leaders' to-do lists, including: Ensuring that your professional staff is up-to-speed on the latest tech changes; setting up students to lead; taking the time to listen to the concerns and issues of parents; and most crucially, setting up teachers for success. Her calls-to-action will have educators cheering: "Now, more than ever before, we need educators and school leaders to be involved in co-constructing the future of education." And her guidance, laced with the daily experience of running a school, brilliantly illustrates just how educators can strap on their pedagogical construction helmets and take charge.

   −Betsy Corcoran | Co-host of the Future Fluent podcast and
   president, d-tech High School.

Dedication

*To all the principals who are doing a difficult job of leading schools.
I see you and thank you.*

*To my family—Mom, Dad, Fivey, Gabriel, Spencer, Phoenix, and Juniper:
I love you!*

To all the educators. We are in this together, and you matter.

Table of Contents

~

Why Leadership Matters in the AI Era

Ignis aurum probat, miseria fortes viros.
"Fire tests gold; adversity tests brave men."
–Seneca, Stoic philosopher of Ancient Rome

S ince the introduction of ChatGPT in November 2022, the need to understand and manage Artificial Intelligence (AI) and Generative AI (GenAI) has drastically increased. For those who are familiar with AI, it seems that literally everyone is talking about some updates or changes that companies like OpenAI and Anthropic are making on a daily basis. There have also been many competing Large Language Models (LLMs), such as ChatGPT, Claude, Gemini, Grok, and DeepSeek, that are competing to capture our attention and, of course, the subscription fees.

Yet, I heard from a colleague of mine, who recently led a workshop for a group of school leaders on AI, that the knowledge level among school leaders varies wildly. Just as many school leaders had varying degrees of competence in technology prior to the pandemic, in this post-pandemic AI world, the variability is astounding.

A 2025 Frontiers in Education survey of school leaders reports that about 50% of school leaders are at the "early-majority" stage of adoption of GenAI, according to roles and seniority, indicating uneven readiness among school leaders rather than uniform competence (Berkovich, 2025)[1]. Such a condition certainly creates a challenge for many educators who are facing the second wave of uncertainty and turmoil after living through the impact of the pandemic.

Why Me?

So, you might wonder what qualifies me to write this book or why you should listen to me. At the risk of sounding arrogant, I like to believe that I have some important and relevant experiences that educators and school leaders might find useful. First of all, I have been fortunate to be in the Learning Science Research space and interact with world-class researchers since 2015, in addition to nearly thirty years of experience as an educator. Since my days of studying learning science at Pepperdine University while earning my Doctorate, I have been involved in various National Science Foundation[2] (NSF) funded projects through Cyberlearning[3] (now CIRCLS)[4], which just ended in 2025.

In 2022, I joined the Practitioner Advisory Board for EngageAI[5] to advise researchers on how to use AI-enabled tools to improve learning. As I write this book, I have continued to support researchers in using AI-enabled tools to enhance teaching and learning. I also became a

---

[1] In this study, Berkovich surveyed 513 principals across three education systems, highlighting differences in readiness by school size and location.

[2] https://www.nsf.gov/

[3] https://www.nsf.gov/funding/opportunities/ritel-research-innovative-technologies-enhanced-learning/nsf17-520/solicitation

[4] https://circls.org/

[5] https://engageai.org/who-we-are/our-team/

Computer Science Teachers Association's 2023-24 Equity Fellow[6] and a Google Innovator in 2024.

I have also been very fortunate to participate in various webinars hosted by the U.S. Department of Education on their launch for the "Artificial Intelligence and the Future of Teaching and Learning[7]," in 2023, and I also participated in a webinar hosted by The Campaign for Grade-Level Reading[8], where Sal Khan introduced Khan Academy's AI-powered tool, Khanamigo for education in 2024.

For the past decade, I have continued to consult on several research projects as a practitioner, particularly as one of the few school principals who speak about the impact of AI in school ecosystems. I also have had professional experience in working with adult learners[9] in looking at data and developing essential skills to become an effective school leader.

Regardless of the space I am in, my focus has always been on supporting my fellow practitioners in gaining access to high-quality, classroom-ready learning technology tools that are validated by rigorous research. Ultimately, my goal has always been to translate high-quality research into actionable steps that can be useful to educators working with the students and families by extension.

Story from the Field: Becoming a School Leader

The longer I am in the learning technology space, the more convinced I am of the importance of leadership. I know that no amount of technology can solve problems without strong and informed leadership in education, which is ironic because I never aspired to be a principal. I

---

[6] https://csteachers.org/2023-24-equity-fellows-instructional-allies/

[7] https://www.ed.gov/sites/ed/files/documents/ai-report/ai-report.pdf

[8] https://www.youtube.com/watch?v=6mCJdrkJWfw

[9] I have taught a doctoral-level statistics course at New Jersey City University for a few years and also trained aspiring administrators through the Santa Barbara County Office of Education for a couple of years.

chose to be "in the arena" as Theodore Roosevelt famously said[10], despite never wanting to be a principal. Because I did not find the leadership I yearned for regarding how I wanted learning technology tools to be implemented in schools when I was not a school leader, I decided to become one and try it myself.

From Tech Coach to Principal

In 2015, I landed what I thought would be my dream job: a district-level Instructional Technology Coach. I was beyond elated. For one blissful year, I spent my days supporting teachers, introducing new tools, and coaching colleagues through tech-enhanced lesson planning. I loved that job so much that I still fantasize about going back to it.

However, one memorable experience I had while in that job set me on a path to becoming a principal. Back then, my job was to bring tools to schools as the Instructional Technology Coach for a large high school district with more than eighteen schools. I remember presenting to a room full of principals. At the time, my district had three teachers on special assignment (TOSAs) for Mathematics, English Language Development (ELD), and Instructional Technology. Earlier in that school year, we were asked to present our work to principals so that they could make important instructional decisions.

First, the math TOSA presented the new instructional strategies that he wanted to pilot to all math teachers in the district using a new type of calculator. After his presentation, the ELD TOSA presented the new reading program that she was hoping all ELD and English teachers would use. Finally, it was my turn to present on the Chromebook pilot that the Instructional Technology Department was hoping to launch. I was proud of the work we were doing until one principal casually stated that he would "wait a few cycles" before deciding whether to participate in the program. Although stated as if he was expressing mere hesitation,

---

[10] Speech at the Sorbonne, Paris, April 23, 1910 by Theodore Roosevelt

it sounded to me like a firm refusal. After hearing from my immediate supervisor that the principal definitely refused to have me come to his school to work with his staff, I was shocked. I didn't realize a single site leader could override what we believed to be a district-wide initiative.

When I asked the IT Director who worked in the District for decades how that was possible, he said, "Because he is the Principal. No one can make a well-respected and beloved principal do something that he refuses to do."

According to the Wallace Foundation Study entitled "How Principals Affect Students and Schools," effective principals have a positive effect on the schools they lead. They contribute to several significant outcomes including student achievement and staff retention (Grissom, Egalite, & Lindsay, 2021). In other words, principals definitely set the tone of the entire school and impact the whole ecosystem.

That single moment changed how I understood the power of site leadership and put me on a path to becoming a high school principal. I learned firsthand how tools, strategies, and plans have little impact if the person in charge of the building doesn't believe in them. Because I believed in getting the right technology tools in the hands of every student I served to help them be prepared for the world yet to be created, I decided to become a principal.

> Tools, strategies, and plans have little impact if the person in charge of the building doesn't believe in them.

Managing Unpredictability: A Leader's Duty

In some ways, today's conversation on AI has a few components of the unpredictable experience that I had during the pandemic shutdown as a site principal. Even with my background in learning technologies, the proliferation of LLMs or GenAI tools and their impact is absolutely new to me and new to all of us: educators and school leaders. Literally every school leader is experiencing the effects of AI in education for the first time as new tools are being created. So, none of us can really rely on the wisdom of the education field, unlike the fortunate leaders of previous generations who could, until the Global Pandemic hit all of us.

Moreover, the impact of AI is broader and more extensive, extending beyond the field of education. As such, the uncertainty around the future can create additional challenges, and it certainly impacts my work as a high school principal.

According to Mathis (2025), the unemployment rate for recent graduates is 5.8%, the highest since 2021. In addition, "College grads are seeking their first jobs. Is AI in the way," included a report by NBC on how "41.2% of new grads are working jobs that don't require their degrees" (Mathis, 2025). In May 2025, *San Francisco Standard* reported that hiring of new graduates by fifteen of the largest tech companies had fallen by more than 50% since 2019 (Jetha & Wallach, 2025). In her *The Atlantic* article entitled, "The Computer-Science Bubble Is Bursting," Horwitch reported that the number of students graduating with a computer science degree at Princeton is set to be twenty-five percent smaller in two years (Horwitch, 2025). Such reports have a significant impact on high schools preparing students for post-secondary education.

As a high school principal, I frequently receive questions from parents regarding what majors graduating seniors should choose, as many graduates with computer science-related degrees struggle to find entry-level positions. I remember speaking with our older son when he was a sophomore at the United States Military Academy at West Point and choosing his major in 2016. He ended up choosing Information Technology (IT) despite my suggestion that he major in Computer Science (CS). I remember him telling me that West Point reduced the number of cadets pursuing CS. Although I can't confirm it, I suspect the Army was already preparing its officers for the arrival of AI even back then.

Since his graduation, our son has been a signal officer in Germany. Although he hasn't shared much about what he does on a daily basis with me, I have heard him speak about working with Palantir[11]. Based on what I know about the company, I know that his work definitely involves using AI. In some ways, he was very fortunate to have been guided on what to study in college.

But what about students at my school? Given that I am responsible for leading a school effectively so that we can equip our graduates for life beyond high school, I can't help but think about the classes we will need to offer to support our students who will be graduating soon and facing such an unpredictable reality. I am sure all school leaders, including my fellow high school principals, are grappling with the responsibility of setting the instructional agenda that is flexible enough for the AI-enabled future.

Site leaders on the front line are expected to be the steady force for our students, thereby serving local communities as we are the people our local constituents trust, despite all the turmoil around us. We are expected to know what to do regardless of what is thrown at us, which can eventually take a toll on leaders.

According to a study conducted by the Rand Corporation (Woo & Steiner, 2022), "just over 80 percent of principals reported 'frequent' feelings of job-related stress, with roughly one-third of principals describing such feelings as 'constant' stress" and the challenges are varied and complex (Love & Lee, 2025, p.2). With over 2200 students and close to 200 staff members currently on our campus, I must admit that there are many days when I don't get to eat or take regular restroom breaks, and I work 12-16 hours straight because I have so many urgent matters to tend to daily. With the advancement of AI, the mix of all

---

[11] https://www.palantir.com/

the challenges I had to manage as a site principal can get exponentially more complex.

Purpose of This Book

After years of participating in national and global conversations on AI, I realized that people want something unique from me when it comes to AI and schools: the voice of the school principals.

Like it or not, as the person at the school building day and night to support staff, students, and families, site principals are ultimately responsible for the whole school in a way that no other person is. Research consistently demonstrates that effective principals exert one of the strongest in-school influences on student outcomes, second only to classroom instruction (Leithwood et al., 2020). Branch, Hanushek, and Rivkin (2013) found that effective principals can raise a typical student's achievement by several months of learning in a single year.

As I learned in my role as district-level technology coach, when you don't have buy-in from the site leader, things don't always get done well or don't get done at all. That's why I decided to become a principal and also to write this book for my fellow principals. I fully understand the impact that my fellow principals can and will have as we navigate the challenges that AI poses in the school ecosystem, and I simply want to share what I have learned.

Let me be very clear: I'm not claiming to be an AI expert. I'm not even claiming to be an expert in leadership. But I am someone who has lived in both the world of research and the reality of schools. I am also a principal who has sat in the seat who had to make final calls at the site level, time and time again, through the pandemic and now in the era of AI. Having spent the last decade trying to connect the dots between what we know from research and what we need in practice, I wanted to share my thoughts on this topic to start the conversation rather than offer an expert opinion.

As such, this book is my way of sharing that journey that I am still on. It's certainly not a prescription or a plan to follow. It is simply a collection of stories, strategies, and questions designed to support my fellow leaders who are trying to make sense of AI and its role in their schools. My goal is to offer a few practical recommendations rooted in useful learning science principles and presented through the lens of someone who is currently leading a school 24-7.

Who This Book Is For

Although I wrote this book specifically for my fellow principals, I hope that others who aspire to become school leaders will find this useful. I would also love to have the general public, who might be interested in learning about what a school leader thinks about when it comes to AI in schools. Finally, I hope that educational technology creators learn about the challenges that a current high school principal is managing so that they can think about creating tools that we need, not what they think we should have.

How to Use This Book

As someone who has been in education for several decades, I know an educator's time is extremely limited and valuable. If you are a site leader, your time is that much more limited. Even if you care a great deal about AI and love to learn more, you often don't have the luxury of reading journals for hours. You can certainly use AI to help you, but how would you know what you are getting is even good or relevant? Most importantly, how would you know to use the knowledge with the group of people you serve day in and day out? I believe you need something you can use immediately, meaningfully, and in context.

I began this book by writing about how I am managing the leadership tension as a high school principal. In Chapter 1, I share what I am personally and professionally grappling with as a site principal when it comes to AI. I included the definitions of AI and a basic framework that I developed with a colleague of mine. In subsequent chapters, I share how I have interacted and continue to interact with different entities and groups of people. I outline my approach to working with the District Office in Chapter 2, teaching staff in Chapter 3, extended staff in Chapter 4, students in Chapter 5, the broader school community, particularly parents, in Chapter 6, and the research field in Chapter 7. I conclude the book with a sense of hope for the future, as I continue to ponder questions about how to be an effective school leader in this new era of AI.

Although I hope you will read the entire book, I have organized it so you can skip directly to a chapter of interest first if you so choose. It is also why each chapter in this book follows the following format:

A Story from the Field

These are my personal and professional stories. I am hoping that you might say, "I know the feeling. That happened to me, too!" or, "That's a good one. I haven't dealt with that, but I think it will be useful," or "Not quite sure what you are talking about, but I dealt with something similar."

I hope my stories resonate with you in a way that makes you feel part of a community of school leaders who must manage a wide range of different situations.

As I describe the relevant events, I have also included my failures, pivots, and lessons learned the hard way. I have shared a few different approaches I've used in response to such challenges at the time. As is always true in real life, some of my choices were good while others were totally ineffectual. But I have always walked away with valuable lessons from each situation.

As you read about my experiences, regardless of whether you think they were successes or a failures, I sincerely hope you will at least laugh with me as I navigate the challenges I call "The Crucible of Leadership[12]" and gather a few nuggets that you will find helpful to refer to as you face similar challenges in your own context.

This section includes relevant research or data that aligns with the lessons I have learned and examples of templates or processes I developed to address an issue.

Recommendations with a Checklist

I end each chapter with a clear set of action steps you can use or adapt. I typically organize these into three tiers, which I call "mild, medium, and spicy" levels: mild for school leaders who are dabbling in AI, medium for school leaders who have some AI knowledge, and spicy for school leaders who consider themselves techies. Because any one of us could be in any one of these levels at any given moment due to the fast-changing AI landscape, my aim is to address as many "levels" in relation to different contexts and groups as possible. Ultimately, my goal is to engage readers by showing how we can support one another.

Following a list of recommendations, I added a checklist for you to consider implementing. This is meant to make your work tangible and practical. In some chapters, these recommendations came from research rather than my own experiences. However, in most chapters, I will share what I have already tried and experienced with some success.

---

[12] As Ethan Hawke wrote in his book Rules for a Knight, "the strongest steel is forged in the hottest fire" (Hawke, 2015, p.1).

Ready to Lead Wrap Up

I have always believed that the purpose of education is to create an educated populace for the protection of democracy. To do so, a leader must hold strong beliefs about what matters in education, such as innovation and inclusion. In fact, I made a bold declaration in front of our staff two years ago that our school would push for full inclusion without fail. While many agreed with the idea, the implementation has been slow and sometimes bumpy.

As idealistic as I might sound based on my definition of the purpose of education, I consider myself to be an absolute pragmatist. I am often hyper-focused on making every situation a win-win for all participants. I wrote this book with that goal: to serve as a no-frills, down-to-earth guide for school leaders who care deeply about their school community but are stretched too thin to spend much time thinking about AI so that we can all be winners.

I always hoped to write a book that I wish I had while working so hard to navigate the new reality, and I hope this is exactly that book for my fellow school leaders.

At its core, this book serves as a conversation starter rather than comprehensive expert advice, because the field is constantly evolving as I write this. I sincerely hope that my fellow school leaders—and aspiring school leaders or educators wondering about what their leaders might be thinking—will ignore many of my shortcomings and focus on a few useful nuggets. So let's get started!

CHAPTER 1

∿

Managing the Tension: Urgency, Strategy, and Soul

"As a principal, you never go and look for an issue. Issues just come to you, and you have no choice but to deal with them."
–Dr. Jeanette Westfall, Retired Assistant Superintendent
of Instruction and Co-Author of *Learner Agency:*
A Field Guide for Taking Flight

Introduction

Leadership in education has always been a complex balancing act. Even before the arrival of GenAI, school leaders navigated competing demands such as juggling between instructional vision and operational realities, innovation and tradition, and staff autonomy and accountability, to name a few. The rapid emergence of AI technology has added layers of complexity, uncertainty, and urgency to an already challenging role.

As a school leader, I rarely seek out problems. In fact, I wish to have the most boring day ever! Unfortunately, problems always seem to catch up with me. A day can start with a text at 5:00 a.m. about how the fire alarm has gone off at school, end with another text at 10:00 p.m. with yet another fire alarm going off, and every unforeseeable challenge in between. New technologies, shifting policies, diverse staff perspectives, and unexpected crises all compete for a school leader's attention daily. The tension between what "should be" and what "is" can feel nearly impossible to get a firm handle on.

> The rapid emergence of AI technology has added layers of complexity, uncertainty, and urgency to an already challenging role.

School leaders know that the trick is to turn that tension into opportunity, which is easier said than done. Unfortunately, practical and actionable solutions are hard to come by when you are mired in the day-to-day. Still, school leaders must get through the day with the mundane while pushing for a vision for the future with AI.

Story from the Field: Just a Typical Day

The following is my schedule for a Friday during the 2nd week of school in the 2024-25 School Year:

Figure 1: Door Sign

I make a habit of posting my daily schedule on a whiteboard on my door, so our staff—or anyone walking by, for that matter—can see where I am and what I am doing at any given moment. Anyone coming by my office can tell what my schedule is like on any given day. So our staff saw what was written above.

However, below is what I actually did during each segment of the day. I have omitted substantive details to protect everyone's privacy, but the table below should provide an overview of my activities on that day:

8:00 a.m.- 8:30 a.m.	Met with the Visual Performing Arts teachers to discuss this year's budget; granted the request to increase funding for one of the classes
8:30 a.m.-9:30 a.m.	Met with the Athletic Director (AD), Chief Business Officer, Physical Education Department Chair, and Assistant Principal (AP) in Charge of Facilities to discuss the Upcoming Gymnasium Renovation Project
9:30 a.m.-10:00 a.m.	Met with the Principal's Assistant (PA) to discuss how to handle an unexpected invoice and a missing field trip request form; later the form was found and sent to the District Office (DO) for approval
10:00 a.m.-10:30 a.m.	Met with a student teacher to sign the form for her assignment and get to know her, learn that she was a heritage speaker who is doing her student teaching for our Spanish for Spanish Speaker Classes
10:30 a.m.-11:00 a.m.	Met with the Teachers' Union President and the AD to discuss concerns regarding a coaching stipend
11:00 a.m.-11:10 a.m.	Supervised the brunch line, picked up trash in the quad after brunch ended, met a freshman student who helped me pick up trash so that I could email his parents to acknowledge and praise his effort
11:10 a.m. - 11:45 a.m.	Met with the Director of Fiscal Services, AP in charge of the Associated Student Body (ASB) to discuss the new accounting procedure for the ASB

11:45 a.m. - 12:30 p.m.	Visited the ASB Students to discuss the logistics of an upcoming school-wide event
12:30 p.m. - 12:45 p.m.	Took a phone call from HR regarding an unexpected vacancy and worked to create a job posting; checked in with a teacher who happened to stop by the office during her prep
12:45 p.m.-1:25 p.m.	Supervised lunch and distributed prizes for a contest that has been running all week long, spoke to a counselor about the Peer Counseling Program that was doing a lunchtime activity, and asked her to make a few adjustments, and walked out to the field to ask several students sitting on the bleachers to return to the main area of the campus for safety reasons
1:25 p.m.-2:00 p.m.	Checked in with a teacher who left campus earlier to visit a doctor because she felt like she had something in her eye that was bothering her, stopped by another class to observe a teacher, and walked into the 3rd teacher's classroom with several newcomers and played a math card game with them for a few minutes
2:00 p.m.-3:00 p.m.	Attended a Zoom call with the community college partners to discuss the Dual Enrollment Partnership
3:00 p.m.-3:30 p.m.	Met a teacher who is interested in advising a Robotics team and the community volunteers to discuss how I can support them to begin working together
3:30 p.m.-4:00 p.m.	Checked in with two APs regarding a teacher's request for changing a student's schedule and answered a few questions from them for the departments that the APs supervise
4:00 p.m.-4:30 p.m.	Sent notification letters on behalf of the administrative team to seventy-two teachers who are to be evaluated this school year

4:30 p.m.-5:30 p.m.	Wrote and sent a Weekly Newsletter to the School Community
5:30 p.m.-5:45 p.m.	Saw a new teacher on my way to the football field and answered a few questions regarding the evaluation process
5:45 p.m.-6:30 p.m.	Attended the Scrimmage game at the football field and brought the cashbox to the Finance Office after the game, along with the AD; checked in with the AD on his mother's health
6:30 p.m.-7:30 p.m.	While driving home, I called two staff members and left a message to let them know what a great job they have been doing
7:30 p.m.-8:30 p.m.	Ate dinner and spent some time with my husband
8:30 p.m.-9:30 p.m.	Edited a video on behalf of the administrative team to share with the staff during our next staff meeting
9:30 p.m.-10:30 p.m.	Read several emails and respond to them.

By looking at the schedule above, you might think that this day was unusually hectic, possibly because it was still early in the school year. However, this day was actually relatively typical because I was able to fit in class visits and interact with several students.

Story from the Field: Never Enough Time

If you asked any school leader, they would all say there is never enough time to get things done that we know to be important and meaningful, such as class visits or checking in with staff members. At a school like mine, with nearly 2,200 students, 150 teachers, 100 support staff members, and 50 coaches, my fellow school leaders and I are fortunate if we can leave our offices to visit classrooms. Don't get me wrong; all five administrators at our site, including myself, constantly push to prioritize class visits and being with the students.

Just to see the types of tasks that I managed, I attempted to keep track of all the items that I handled daily in the 2023-24 school year. I quickly realized that I didn't have the time to track all the tasks on a daily basis, despite my best efforts. So I ended up relying on my calendar and a notebook with a scribbled list to keep track of what I needed to accomplish.

In an ideal scenario, an AI assistant tool could be an answer. After all, I frequently use apps that record my voice and convert the recordings into text. The web is filled with such recommendations, and I am encouraged to see that there is an effort to create useful productivity tools for busy professionals. However, GenAI tools are not yet where we would like them to be.

For example, one of my assistant principals has used Fyxer AI to automate her email response since May of 2024. Currently priced at $270 per year for an individual user, it costs about the same as ChatGPT, Claude, or Gemini, which I am using to see if they are helpful in my work. So I tested FlyxerAI[13] out for a week to see if I liked it. One reason I decided to try it was that Fyxer is a technology company located in London. Due to Europe's General Data Protection Regulation (GDPR)[14] and Fyxer's disclaimer of meeting the Health Insurance Portability and Accountability Act (HIPAA)[15] regulations, I felt it was worth a try.

---

[13] www.fyxer.com

[14] GDPR stands for General Data Protection Regulation, a European law that protects people's personal data including any information that can identify someone such as their name, email, photo, or even an IP address (GDPR.eu, n.d.) GDPR gives individuals control over their own data and tells organizations how they can collect, use, store, and share it responsibly.

[15] HIPAA stands for the Health Insurance Portability and Accountability Act of 1996 that protects sensitive patient health information (PHI) (U.S. Department of Health & Human Services, n.d.).

During the initial week, however, I found myself having to stop what I was doing to answer Fyxer's questions or having to edit or actively ignore its constant recommendations. So I stopped the trial after a week. However, I began using it again at the start of this new school year. I find the tool to be useful in categorizing various emails quickly, rather than having to use the email filter native to Gmail that our district uses as its primary email tool. Still, I spend a lot of time having to edit FyxerAI-generated emails. In addition, it has miscategorized and filtered several emails, including an email from my IT director or a parent more than once, which delayed my responses. So I am on the fence as to whether the tool is actually saving me time.

Reality Check: More Time Spent Learning to Use the Tools than Receiving Benefits from Using Them

As you can see from the example above, every time you are introduced to a new tool, you must invest time in learning how to use the tool. When it comes to implementing a new AI tool, any experienced school leader will tell you that the opportunity cost has to be great for them to start using a new tool. In my case, I didn't think it was worth it yet, and that is the case with many AI tools at the moment. Because of that, many school leaders are hesitant to invest their precious time in using a new AI tool for their school, based on how quickly these tools appear to become obsolete.

Yet the statistics seem to push towards school leaders needing to reconsider how they are approaching AI in their schools. According to RAND Corporation's April 17, 2024 report, only 18% of K-12 teachers reported using AI for teaching despite the fall of 2023 (Diliberti, Schwartz, Doan, Shapiro, Rainey, & Lake, 2024). In 2025, however, the Stanford Human-Centered Artificial Intelligence reported that 78% of businesses reported using AI and 71% reported using GenAI

(Kariuki, 2025, p. 220), and the latest finding published by the Rand Corporation showed that 53% of the surveyed teachers have used AI for schools (Doss et al., 2025). Regardless of which statistics you trust, the trend is clear. More educators are using and will use AI in order to improve their practices, and school leaders must respond to this trend.

Key Findings

+ In 2025, 54 percent of students and 53 percent of English language arts, math, and science teachers indicated that they used AI for school. These are increases of more than 15 percentage points compared with survey results in the past one to two years.

+ More high school than middle school students reported using AI for school, and progressively higher percentages of elementary, middle, and high school teachers said that they used AI during the school year.

+ Sixty-one percent of parents, 48 percent of middle schoolers, 55 percent of high schoolers, and only 22 percent of district leaders agreed that greater use of AI will harm students' critical-thinking skills.

+ Half of students said that they are worried they will be falsely accused of using AI to cheat.

+ As of spring 2025, 35 percent of district leaders reported that they provide students with training on AI.

+ Over 80 percent of students reported that teachers did not explicitly teach them how to use AI for schoolwork.

+ Forty-five percent of principals reported having school or district policies or guidance on the use of AI in schools, and 34 percent of teachers reported having school or district policies on the use of AI related to academic integrity.

(Doss et al., Sep. 30. 2025)

What Do You Mean by AI?

Before I recommend what my fellow school leaders should do with all these AI tools, I want to clarify what most teachers think when they hear the term "AI." I subscribe to the following definition for educators from the EducatorCIRCLS website:

> More educators are using and will use AI in order to improve their practices, and school leaders must respond to this trend.

> AI is a branch of computer science. **AI systems use hardware, algorithms, and data to create "intelligence" to do things like make decisions, discover patterns, and perform some sort of action.** AI is a general term and there are more specific terms used in the field of AI. AI systems can be built in different ways, two of the primary ways are: (1) through the use of rules provided by a human (rule-based systems); or (2) with machine learning algorithms. Many newer AI systems use machine learning (see definition of machine learning below). (Ruiz, P., & Fusco, J., 2024).

A more simplistic definition can be found in the seminal document "Artificial Intelligence and the Future of Teaching and Learning: Insights and Recommendations," published by the US Department of Education's Office of Educational Technology.

> **AI can be defined as "automation based on associations."** When computers automate reasoning based on associations in data (or associations deduced from expert knowledge), two shifts fundamental to AI occur and shift computing beyond conventional edtech: (1) from capturing data to detecting patterns in data and (2) from providing access to instructional resources to automating decisions about

instruction and other educational processes. Detecting patterns and automating decisions are leaps in the level of responsibilities that can be delegated to a computer system. (U.S. Department of Education, Office of Educational Technology, 2023, p. 1)

However, many educators tend to think of AI in terms of specific tools that can be used to perform tasks. For example, a teacher recently shared with me that she was using Class Companion[16] for her Advanced Placement (AP) European class. She was excited to report that her students were receiving instant feedback on their responses to various short-answer questions and really honing their writing skills. Another teacher reported that he used Brisk[17] to create multiple-choice questions for his students because he wanted them to read a new short story in Spanish. A third teacher reported that she used Brisk to modify the Lexile level of a text for her English Language Learners (ELLs) so that the text was much more accessible.

Despite the fact that AI has been around for several decades[18], the release of ChatGPT in 2022 has caused educators to view AI to be synonymous with ChatGPT or similar tools that are built on OpenAI. Such mislabeling is concerning, because the specificity of language matters when making important decisions, such as whether to bring a tool into our school ecosystem or not. However, busy educators don't necessarily have time to think about the precision of definitions. I sometimes wonder if I have the time to think about that myself.

Still, I encourage my fellow school leaders to model the way in elevating the conversation by becoming aware of the definitions of AI and how they are being used by staff members they supervise, as

---

[16] https://classcompanion.com/

[17] https://www.briskteaching.com/

[18] Many consider Alan Turing to be the Father of Artificial Intelligence due to the Turing Test that he proposed in his 1950 article "Computing Machinery and Intellconsiderhaveigence" (Turing, 1950).

well as the general school community. Here are two useful graphics for anyone to consider when thinking about what we mean by AI in our daily conversations.

The first graphic illustrates the position of LLMs, such as ChatGPT, Claude, or Gemini, within the field of computing. As you can see, to refer to these LLMs as AI is actually a misrepresentation of the actual AI field that includes other disciplines such as machine learning, deep learning, natural language processing, data mining, and big data that has roots in the general computer science field, which also includes some aspects of data mining and big data. Yet, we have begun using AI to represent a very small segment of what we considered to be computer science.

What is AI?

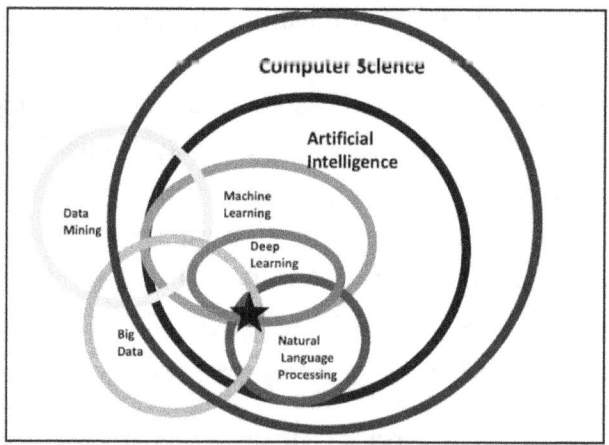

Figure by Judy Fusco and Pati Ruiz
Glossary of AI Terms for Educators

Figure 2: What is an AI? (Ruiz and Fusco, 2025)

The second graphic represents all the specific tasks or functions that each subfield of study specializes in. As you can see below, even though AI can do many things, a single tool can't do all the things and do them well because of the way that programming works.

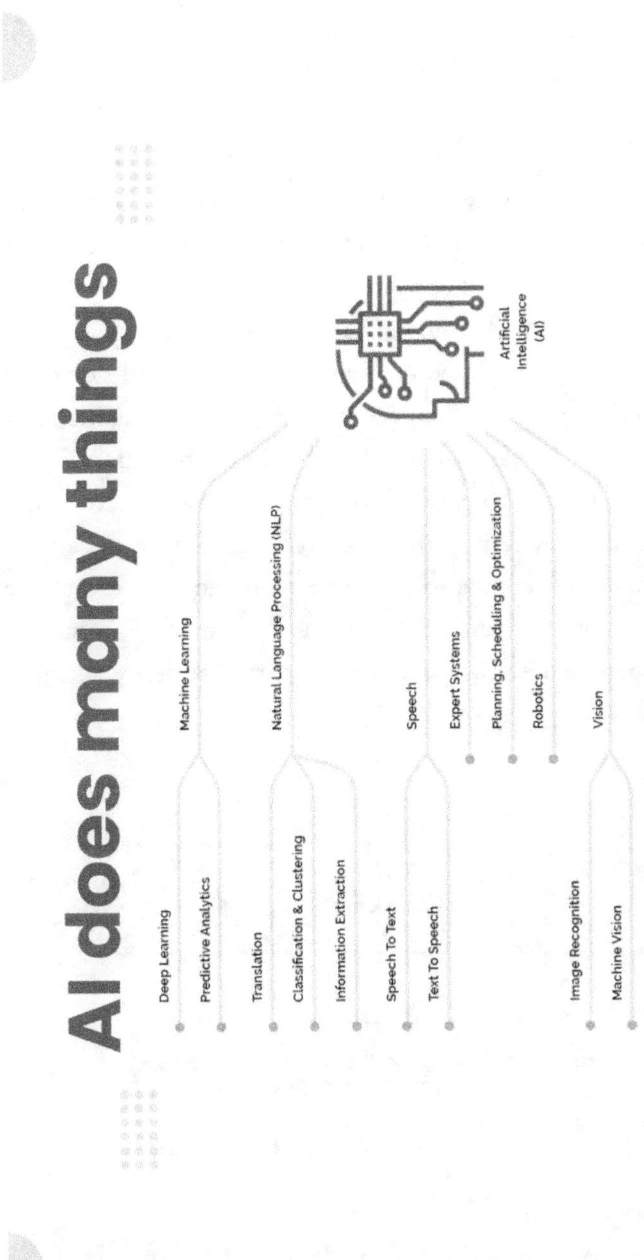

AI does many things

Deep Learning

Machine Learning

Predictive Analytics

Translation

Natural Language Processing (NLP)

Classification & Clustering

Information Extraction

Speech To Text

Speech

Text To Speech

Expert Systems

Planning, Scheduling & Optimization

Robotics

Image Recognition

Vision

Machine Vision

Artificial Intelligence (AI)

Introduction to Artificial Intelligence (AI): A Deep Dive into Machine Learning & Deep Learning | by BangBit Technologies | Medium

Figure 3: AI does many things (BangBit Technologies, 2018)

I have used these two graphics at the start of my presentations recently to emphasize the importance of the specificity of terms when we talk about AI and to manage the expectations of what each tool can do for educators.

Arthur Clarke once said, "Any sufficiently advanced technology is indistinguishable from magic" (1973, p. 21). As we continue to observe the development of AI, we might succumb to the belief that AI is doing something magical beyond our comprehension. However, we must remember that it is a human-created tool. As such, we must guard against engaging in a type of mental offloading as leaders. In fact, it is now more important than ever to know that (1) LLMs, now commonly referred to as AI, is a small part of a large computer science field, and (2) a specific field of study is designed to produce a tool that can perform specific function well; therefore, a human must be fully engaged in selecting different tools for different purposes to get the desired outcomes for the benefit of humans. For instance, a human must give a comprehensive prompt to the tool to get the desired output, as illustrated below.

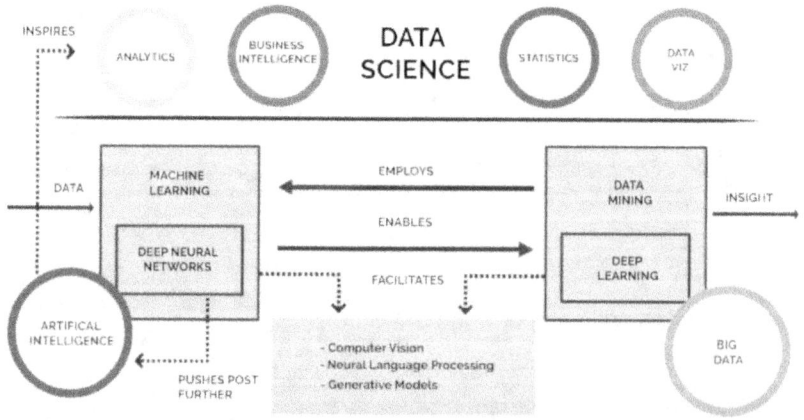

Figure 4: AI Adaptive Software (BangBit Technologies, 2018)

The Use Cases: Prompting and Communicating

So what would help a school leader like you and me when everyone on campus is looking at you to be the solution-giver? I have asked ChatGPT, Claude, and Gemini this very question. To assist this, I constructed the following prompts. The first prompt was created based on the SPARK[19] Framework developed by Sabba Quidwai and the Four Pillar Structure recommended by OpenAI President Greg Brockman[20].

Prompt 1:

As a high school principal, I find it challenging to navigate the uncertainty of an ever-changing AI landscape and its impact on my students' future plans. I aspire to be an inspirational guide for my fellow principals with a utilitarian lens. I would love a list of practical recommendations that are immediately implementable for any school leader. Give me a list of five recommendations.

---

[19] SPARK represents Situation, Problem, Aspiration, Results, and Kismet (Quidwai, 2024).

[20] The Four Pillars includes Goal, Return Format, Warning, and Context Dump (Brockman, 2025).

ChatGPT said:

Here are **five immediately actionable recommendations** for school leaders who want to navigate the uncertain AI landscape with both *inspiration and pragmatism*—a blend of vision and utility.

1. Establish a "Human-Centered AI Literacy" Framework

Assumption: AI literacy should start with technical skills.

Counterpoint: The most valuable starting point is *ethical and human understanding.*

Actionable Step:

Launch a monthly "AI in Real Life" staff series where teachers analyze case studies on AI bias, authorship, or misinformation. Use the framework:

- *What can AI do?*
- *What should humans still do?*
- *What happens if we don't discern between the two?*
  This cultivates AI literacy that's *values-driven*, not just tool-driven.

2. Create a "Future Pathways Council" with Students

Assumption: Students are passive recipients of AI's changes.
Counterpoint: They are your best co-researchers.
Actionable Step:
Invite a small, diverse group of students to meet quarterly with counselors and industry mentors to explore emerging AI-related careers, ethics, and civic issues. Publish their findings in your school newsletter.

→ *Outcome:* You turn uncertainty into student agency.

---

3. Pilot a "Low-Stakes AI Use Policy" for Staff

Assumption: AI implementation requires a formal district policy first.
Counterpoint: Waiting for perfection stifles innovation.
Actionable Step:
Start with a **"sandbox policy"**—allow teachers to experiment with AI for lesson planning or communication under clear boundaries (e.g., no confidential data, student identifiers, or grading).

Debrief monthly to collect best practices before formalizing site-wide policy.

→ *Outcome:* Staff feel empowered, not policed.

4. Audit Your Curriculum for "AI-Resilient Skills"

Assumption: AI replaces the need to teach foundational skills.
Counterpoint: It heightens their importance.
Actionable Step:
Ask each department to identify which parts of their curriculum:

* Should **leverage** AI (efficiency, ideation, analysis)
* Should **resist** AI (critical reading, ethics, reasoning)

Hold a cross-department meeting to realign around skills that endure: communication, collaboration, and discernment.

→ *Outcome:* The curriculum evolves strategically, not reactively.

5. Model AI Transparency and Ethical Leadership

Assumption: Leaders must appear certain about AI to inspire confidence.

Counterpoint: Modeling *curiosity and transparency* builds more trust than false certainty.

Actionable Step:
In your weekly memo or staff meeting, share one AI tool you tested, how you evaluated it, and what ethical question it raised for you. Invite open critique.

→ *Outcome:* You normalize adaptive leadership and collective sense-making.

Claude said:

Here are five practical recommendations you can implement immediately to help your students navigate the AI-transformed future:

1. Integrate AI literacy across existing curricula rather than treating it as a separate subject. Start by having teachers incorporate basic AI tools into their current lessons - English teachers can explore AI writing assistants for drafting and revision exercises, math teachers can demonstrate computational thinking through AI problem-solving examples, and history teachers can discuss AI's societal implications. This approach requires no new courses or major budget allocations while ensuring every student gains foundational AI understanding regardless of their academic track.

2. Establish "Human Skills Fridays" or similar regular programming focused on capabilities AI cannot replicate. Dedicate time each week to developing critical thinking, emotional intelligence, creative problem-solving, and interpersonal communication through structured activities like Socratic seminars, peer mediation training, design thinking workshops, or collaborative projects. These sessions can be run by existing staff using free resources and directly address employers' growing emphasis on distinctly human competencies that complement AI tools.

3. Create AI disclosure and ethics policies that mirror real-world professional standards. Rather than banning AI tools, teach students to use them responsibly by requiring citation of AI assistance, establishing clear guidelines about appropriate versus inappropriate use, and having students reflect on their AI interactions. This prepares them for college and workplace environments where AI use is expected but must be transparent and ethical, while also teaching critical evaluation of AI-generated content.

4. Launch student-led "AI exploration committees" that research and present on emerging tools and their applications. Give students ownership of their learning by having rotating groups investigate new AI developments and share findings with peers and faculty through brief monthly presentations. This costs nothing, builds research and presentation skills, keeps your school current with rapid AI changes, and empowers students to become active participants in their technological future rather than passive recipients.

5. Develop partnerships with local businesses and colleges for "AI in Action" visits or virtual sessions. Contact nearby companies, universities, and community colleges to arrange presentations showing how AI is actually being used in various fields - from healthcare to manufacturing to creative industries. These partnerships require only coordination time, provide students with concrete career pathway insights, and help them understand that AI augments rather than replaces human workers in most fields, reducing anxiety while building practical awareness.

These recommendations require minimal resources while maximizing benefit across your entire student body, embodying the utilitarian approach you're seeking while remaining immediately actionable.

Gemini said:

Here are five practical, high-utility recommendations for school leaders to navigate the impact of AI.

1. Assemble a Standing "AI Task Force" (Don't Just Update a Policy)

Instead of a top-down policy that's outdated in six months, create a small, standing committee.

- **Who:** Include an administrator, two tech-savvy teachers, one skeptical teacher, a librarian/media specialist, and (most importantly) two or three students.
- **Utility:** This group's job isn't just to write rules. It's to be the school's "sense-making" body. They meet briefly every month to discuss new tools, share what's working (and what's not) in classrooms, and propose *iterative* updates to your academic integrity guidelines.
- **Immediate Action:** Send the email to form this group today. Frame it as an "exploratory committee" to lower the stakes and encourage participation.

2. Run "Show, Don't Tell" Teacher PD

Teachers are overwhelmed. Another mandatory "how-to" session on a new tool will be met with resistance. The utilitarian approach is to show immediate, practical value.

- **What:** Host a **peer-led "AI Playground" session** during your next staff meeting. Ask a few willing teachers (one from Humanities, one from STEM) to share *one* specific way AI has saved them time.
- **Example:** Show how they used an AI tool to generate five different versions of a text for differentiated reading levels, or how they used it to brainstorm lesson-planning ideas.

- **Immediate Action:** Identify your "early adopter" teachers this week and ask them to share for 10 minutes at the next meeting. Focus entirely on **teacher workload reduction**—this provides the greatest immediate benefit and builds buy-in for student-facing changes later.

3. Re-brand "AI Literacy" as "Modern Research"

Don't create a new "AI Class." Instead, integrate AI skills into the classes you already have, primarily through your English and Social Studies departments.

- **Utility:** Students are already using AI to write essays. Banning it is futile. The most practical solution is to teach them how to use it as a *tool*, not a *crutch*.
- **What:** Train teachers to focus on **AI-assisted brainstorming, critical evaluation, and citation.**
- **Immediate Action:** Provide teachers with a simple framework. For the next research paper, require students to submit their "AI conversation transcript" (their prompts and the AI's answers) as part of their appendix. The grade shifts from *just* the final essay to the *process* of inquiry—how they fact-checked the AI, refined their questions, and built upon the initial ideas.

4. Champion "AI-Proof" Assessments

If an AI can complete the assignment, it's probably not a great assignment. This is a powerful, utilitarian lever you can pull as an instructional leader.

- **Utility:** This shifts the focus from "catching cheaters" to "designing better learning&
- **What:** Publicly and privately champion assessments that AI struggles with. These include:
  - **In-class discussions** and Socratic seminars.
  - **Group collaboration** and project-based learning.
  - **Hands-on labs** and real-world problem-solving.

> Personal reflection and connecting course content to their own lives.
>
> + **Immediate Action:** In your next faculty newsletter or meeting, highlight one example of an "AI-proof" assignment a teacher is already doing. Ask your department chairs to have their teams brainstorm one way to "human-proof" one major assessment this semester.
>
> **5. Host a "Future of Work" Parent Town Hall (with Students)**
>
> Much of the friction and fear comes from parents who are confused about what this means for their child's future.
>
> + **Utility:** You provide a massive service to your community by cutting through the media hype and grounding the conversation in practical reality.
> + **What:** Host a 60-minute virtual or in-person town hall. Don't just focus on "cheating& Frame it around **"How We're Preparing Your Child for an AI-Powered World&**
> + **Immediate Action:** Schedule the event. Invite your new "AI Task Force" (from #1) to be on the panel. Have a student show (safely) how they use AI to study. Reassure parents that the core skills—critical thinking, creativity, and collaboration—are now more important than ever, and that is the school's central focus.

Prompt 2:

Provide me with a list of five practical recommendations for a school leader in implementing AI at their school. Organize the recommendations for three types of AI users: novice, intermediate, and highly-skilled. Do not include any generic or vague recommendations. I am an experienced high school principal who is sharing these recommendations with other school leaders.

ChatGPT said:

Here are **five concrete recommendations** for school leaders implementing AI, organized by three user-levels (novice, intermediate, highly-skilled). Since you're an experienced high-school principal, I'll aim each recommendation at actionable practice rather than generic "get buy-in" phrasing.

Novice AI Users (staff or school leaders who are just beginning)

1. Run a short "AI-tool sandbox" pilot

- Select one accessible generative AI tool (e.g., a teacher uses ChatGPT or a teacher-edition AI planner) for one department for 4–6 weeks.

- Set clear goals: e.g., "use AI to produce 3 lesson-plan drafts in 30 minutes and refine them with teacher input."

- After pilot, collect teacher feedback: What worked? What didn't? What concerns emerged? This aligns with the "pilot testing" phase in district AI guidance. (Los Angeles County Office of Education)

- Why this works: It avoids large-scale rollout before staff feel comfortable; it builds early wins and surfaces common questions.

2. Create a "trustworthy-AI checklist" for procurement/use

- Develop a simple one-page checklist for any AI tool: Does it comply with your district's privacy/FERPA policy? Has student data been anonymized? Can a teacher override the AI output? What vendor transparency exists?

+ This is rooted in guidance stressing compliance, human-agency and evaluation of AI tools. (Policy Analysis for California Education)

+ Implementation: Make it part of any vendor contract or teacher request for an AI tool. Post the checklist on your school intranet so it becomes visible.

3. Launch a "What is AI? What it's not?" staff learning micro-session

+ With perhaps a department meeting, run a 30-minute session: define AI vs automation vs data analytics; highlight a misuse scenario (e.g., entering student Personally Identifiable Information into a generative-AI prompt) and a best-practice scenario (teacher uses AI to generate adaptive questions, then edits).

+ This builds foundational literacy, which is a recurring principle in the national and international guidance. (World Economic Forum)

+ Tip: End session with two teacher "commitments" – one concrete (e.g., "I will try AI to generate exit tickets by next Friday") and one reflective (e.g., "I will note how AI output differed from my original thinking").

4. Embed AI use into one existing initiative rather than starting a new one

+ For example: take your school's staff-wellbeing initiative and incorporate "AI-assistant for staff scheduling" rather than launching a separate "AI initiative."

+ Why: Leveraging existing work lowers change-fatigue, helps staff see AI as support rather than a new burden.

+ You'll then track: Did the AI tool reduce scheduling time? Did staff feel more empowered or less? Use that data to make the case for next steps.

5. Draft a simple "AI use" addendum to your school's Acceptable Use Policy (AUP)

+ With your legal/IT team, add language: e.g., "Use of generative-AI tools must not substitute the student's original work unless explicitly approved," "Staff must treat AI output as draft, apply human judgment and verify facts," "Student data must not be entered into AI prompts unless anonymized." (CESA 6)

+ Implementation: Communicate to staff, students and parents via newsletter, include a short summary at back-to-school night, and link to the full policy on the school website.

Intermediate AI Users (those who have used AI in some capacities and are ready to scale)

Intermediate AI Users (those who have used AI in some capacities and are ready to scale)

1. Map AI-supported workflows across instruction, operations and equity-goals

+ Create a matrix: columns = school functions (instruction/ planning, student-support-services, operations like scheduling/HR), rows = AI-opportunity, current status, next step, owner.

+ Example: Instruction row: "Adaptive question-bank generation" → current status: pilot in 2 teachers; next step: scale to 6 teachers this semester; owner: instructional coach.

+ This aligns with guidance to build strategy that fits student/ teacher needs and operations. (K-12 Dive)

+ Ensure one row is dedicated to "equity & access" (e.g., use AI to analyze access gaps, personalize remediation) so you avoid only automating existing inequities.

2. Create teacher-AI co-design teams (teacher + ed-tech + student voice)

+ Form 2 or 3 cross-functional teams that meet bi-weekly for one semester, charged with (a) identifying one pain point in teaching or operations, (b) designing an AI-augmented workflow, (c) measuring its impact and refining.

+ The inclusion of student voice and teacher agency is emphasized in filtered policy guidance. (National Education Association)

+ As principal, you could attend one of the sessions to signal priority and learn frontline issues.

3. Design prompt-literacy learning modules for teaching staff and advanced students

+ Move beyond "try AI" to "craft prompts". Develop three prompt categories: (1) Creative brainstorming (2) Data-analysis or analytics prompts (3) Instructional design prompts (lesson plan scaffolding, differentiation). Provide exemplar prompts and ask staff to refine them, then test the output.

+ This addresses the literacy gap in teacher and student use of generative-AI. (arXiv)

+ Monitor: track how many teachers revise the generated outputs vs accept them verbatim.

4. Implement a "metadata logging & review" protocol for AI tool use across classes

+ Require teachers using AI tools to log: what tool, what prompt, how they edited output, time saved, student feedback. Quarterly review by instructional leadership.

+ Why: This builds data on ROI, supports reflection and continuous improvement (key principle: evaluation). (Policy Analysis for California Education)

+ Use this data as part of your end-of-year reflection and planning for next year's AI strategy.

5. Develop a student-facing "AI Literacy & Responsibility Badge Program"

+ Create levels (Bronze/Silver/Gold) for students: Bronze = understand what AI is and responsible use; Silver = design prompts for learning; Gold = lead peer workshops or use AI for capstone project.

+ This aligns student agency with your instructional vision, ensures students aren't passive recipients but active users of AI.

+ Tie badge achievements to school communications/newsletter so it becomes part of culture and encourages peer-leadership.

Highly-Skilled AI Users (leaders/staff proficient in AI workflows and looking to transform practice)

1. Use AI-driven data analytics for predictive student-support systems, with human-in-the-loop oversight

- For example: use an AI model to flag patterns of assignment non-completion, participation dips, normalized across demographics, then assign a student-support coordinator to conduct human interview.

- Critical: human-decision-making must remain central (a key principle in AI guidance). (<u>Policy Analysis for California Education</u>)

- You should monitor for bias in model inputs and ensure transparency (e.g., why a student was flagged). Document the process and results for continuous governance.

2. Partner with an external vendor/academic to co-design domain-specific AI tools tailored to your school's pedagogy

- Instead of off-the-shelf only, engage a vendor or university researcher to build an AI module specific to your school's instructional model (for example, analyzing student writing over time and giving individualized next-step suggestions aligned with your rubric).

- Since many tools are generic, a custom approach allows richer integration. But you'll need contract terms covering data-privacy, vendor transparency, model auditability (aligned with global guidance). (<u>U.S. Department of Education</u>)

+ Roll-out in phases: prototype with single grade, refine, scale.

3. Institute a formal "AI ethics & governance committee" with student, teacher, parent, IT and legal representation

+ Set quarterly meetings to review new tools, revisit policies, handle misuse incidents, audit data-security, evaluate equity-metrics (who's using AI, who's excluded).

+ Governance is a key emerging need in K–12 AI implementation. (arXiv)

+ As principal, you chair it for the first year: publish an annual summary visible on the school website.

4. Embed AI-enhanced personalized learning paths that integrate human mentoring and monitor impact

+ For high-achieving and historically under-performing students alike, design AI-driven branching pathways: the AI suggests modules, scaffolds student work, teacher mentors jump in at decision-points. Track growth (academic, social-emotional) over semesters.

+ The idea: AI augments human mentorship, not replaces it. Literature warns against AI displacing cognitive effort. (arXiv)

+ Use this as a case-study internally (and perhaps for your speaking/consulting work) to show measurable outcomes.

5. Publish and present your school's AI-implementation story (with data) at district/state/national level

- Since you have your brand and network, document your process (pilot→scale→governance→impact), prepare a one-page executive summary, a slide deck for principals, and a podcast/blog entry.

- This adds to the field's capacity (others often reinvent), and positions your school as a leader. It also helps you reflect critically on what worked and what didn't—an essential part of continuous improvement.

Claude said:

Here are five practical recommendations for implementing AI in your school, organized by user skill level:

For Novice AI Users

Start with structured AI writing feedback tools in English and Language Arts classes. Rather than jumping into open-ended AI use, begin with platforms like Grammarly Education or Turnitin's AI writing feedback features that provide controlled, specific feedback on student writing. Have teachers pilot these tools with one assignment type first, such as argumentative essays, and establish clear protocols for when students should use AI feedback versus teacher feedback. This gives both teachers and students experience with AI in a bounded, educationally-focused context while building comfort with the technology.

Implement AI-assisted formative assessment tools in math departments. Deploy platforms like Khan Academy's Khanmigo or Carnegie Learning's MATHia that use AI to provide personalized practice problems and immediate feedback. These tools don't require teachers to understand AI deeply but offer clear pedagogical benefits. Set up weekly data review meetings where math teachers examine the AI-generated progress reports together, helping them learn to interpret and act on AI-provided insights while supporting each other through the learning curve.

For Intermediate AI Users

Establish interdisciplinary AI project teams for curriculum enhancement. Create teams of 3-4 teachers from different departments who meet biweekly to develop AI-enhanced lesson plans and share what works. For example, pair a history teacher using AI for primary source analysis with a science teacher using it for data visualization. Provide these teams with dedicated planning time and a shared Google Drive folder of successful AI prompts and lesson templates. This cross-pollination approach accelerates skill development while ensuring AI integration isn't siloed by department.

For Highly-Skilled AI Users

Deploy these teachers as AI integration coaches with formal responsibilities. Rather than relying on informal peer support, designate your AI-proficient teachers as official AI Integration Coaches with one period of release time dedicated to this role. Have them conduct monthly workshops on advanced topics like prompt engineering for differentiated instruction, using AI for authentic assessment design, or creating custom GPTs for specific curricular needs. Task them with maintaining a school-wide AI resource hub and conducting quarterly audits of AI tool effectiveness across departments.

Pioneer advanced AI applications in specialized programs. Have your most skilled users lead pilot programs in areas like using AI for IEP goal tracking and progress monitoring in special education, developing AI-powered simulations for AP science courses, or creating AI assistants that help counselors with college application essay review. Document these pilots thoroughly with clear metrics for success, creating case studies that can guide broader implementation. These advanced users should present their findings at faculty meetings quarterly, demonstrating concrete educational outcomes rather than just technical capabilities.

These recommendations move beyond general "explore AI" advice to provide specific entry points and progression paths that acknowledge the varied skill levels in your building while maintaining focus on educational outcomes rather than technology for its own sake.

Gemini said:

Here are five practical, non-generic recommendations for implementing AI, structured for your fellow school leaders and broken down by the skill level of their staff.

1. Reframe Academic Integrity from "Gotcha" to "Glass Box"

The goal is to move from a punitive "cheating" model to a transparent "process" model.

- **For Novice Users:** Implement a **"Cite Your AI" policy**. This is the most immediate and practical first step. Require all students and staff to add a simple citation or footnote describing *how* they used an AI tool (e.g., "Used ChatGPT 4.0 to brainstorm an outline and refine paragraph transitions"). This normalizes use while maintaining accountability.
- **For Intermediate Users:** Develop **"AI Process-Check" assignments**. Instead of just grading the final product, have students submit their AI prompts, the AI's initial output, and a brief reflection on how they edited, fact-checked, and improved the AI's work. This shifts the graded skill from *writing* to *critical editing and augmentation.*
- **For Highly-Skilled Users:** Mandate **"Human-in-the-Loop" verification** for all staff. For example, if a department uses AI to analyze student data, they must submit a "Verification Addendum" detailing how they checked the AI's conclusions for bias or statistical errors. This builds critical oversight into all high-level administrative work.

2. Prioritize Productivity PD Before Pedagogical PD

Teachers are overwhelmed. The fastest way to get buy-in is to give them time back *first*, before asking them to change *how* they teach.

- **For Novice Users:** Host a 60-minute, optional workshop focused *only* on **teacher administrative tasks.** Demonstrate 3-5 specific prompts for generating differentiated parent emails, creating meeting agendas from bullet points, and scaffolding basic lesson plan components.
- **For Intermediate Users:** Create a shared prompt library for **differentiating instructional materials.** Show teachers how to use AI to instantly generate five versions of a single text for different reading levels, create leveled exit tickets, or modify word problems for varied learning needs.
- **For Highly-Skilled Users:** Fund a small cohort of "AI Innovators" to develop and share **advanced productivity workflows.** This could involve using AI to analyze school-wide assessment data to identify intervention groups or building a custom GPT trained on your school's curriculum maps to assist new teachers.

3. Create a "Vetted Tool Sandbox," Not a Free-for-All

Instead of banning everything or allowing anything, create a controlled environment that protects student data and focuses efforts.

- **For Novice Users:** Establish a **"Red Light, Green Light" list** published on the school intranet. "Green" tools are ones you've vetted for data privacy (FERPA/COPPA compliance) and allowlisted. "Red" tools are known to have data privacy issues or are not curriculum-aligned. This provides immediate clarity.
- **For Intermediate Users:** Empower department heads to pilot *one* new AI tool per semester. Provide them with a **formal "Tool Vetting Rubric"** (questions on data policy, pedagogical value, cost) and have them present their findings—and a usage recommendation—to the leadership team.
- **For Highly-Skilled Users:** Implement a **centralized AI dashboard or portal** (like a single sign-on page) that provides access *only* to institutionally approved and licensed tools. This allows you to manage licenses, control data, and gather usage metrics to evaluate ROI.

4. Move from Broad Policy to Specific Task Rubrics

A high-level Acceptable Use Policy (AUP) is necessary but insufficient. Teachers and students need to know what "use" looks like for a *specific assignment*.

- **For Novice Users:** Co-create a simple **"AI Use by Task-Type" chart** with your staff. For example:
  - **Brainstorming:** Encouraged
  - **First Draft:** Permitted, with citation
  - **Editing/Grammar:** Encouraged
  - **In-Class Essay:** Not permitted
- **For Intermediate Users:** Ask departments to create **assignment-specific AI rubrics.** A history research paper rubric, for example, could have a row for "Effective and Ethical Use of AI," with points awarded for using AI to find diverse primary sources vs. points deducted for "hallucinated" citations.
- **For Highly-Skilled Users:** Task teams with developing **AI-resistant assessment models.** This involves shifting assessments from simple recall (which AI excels at) to tasks requiring in-class argumentation, real-time problem-solving, synthesis of novel data, or oral defense of a submitted product.

5. Launch a Student-Facing "Digital Citizen" Task Force

Don't just talk *about* students; include them. Their perspective is critical for identifying the real-world ethical challenges and opportunities they face.

- **For Novice Users:** Run a **student-led assembly or advisory lesson** where students demonstrate *how* they are using AI tools (both for good and for shortcuts). Use this as a listening session to inform your most immediate policy needs.
- **For Intermediate Users:** Create a formal **"Student AI Ethics Council"** that meets quarterly. Present them with real-world scenarios (e.g., "A student uses AI to create art for a contest," "A student uses AI to summarize a book they didn't read") and

have them help craft the school's response.
- **For Highly-Skilled Users:** Partner your student task force with a local university or tech company to engage in **real-world AI literacy projects**. Have them investigate and present to the school board on topics like algorithmic bias in platforms they use or the future of AI in careers they want to pursue.

I hope you can see how each model responded differently, yet there is definitely a pattern to these answers. Some of the recommendations are not only doable but quite practical. How do I know? Because I have already tried and succeeded in implementing a few activities included in the answers above.

Another use case that I think might be helpful is the ability to use an AI tool to craft standardized messages that any school leader can send to their school community. For example, I asked Gemini to craft a Halloween-related message for our school community, reminding the student body that all school rules, including dress code expectations and attendance requirements, still applied even on Halloween. I have also used ChatGPT to help me craft a message regarding a lockdown drill.

An LLM can generate starter messages that are useful If the task is routine and standardized. However, I edited at least 75% of what was generated, even when I have asked for a message to remind our community about the upcoming earthquake drill. Still, I keep trying to see if Gemini will read my mind and write just like me someday, since I often import what Gemini has created to a Google Doc and edit. I have also asked ChatGPT to reformat the citations or give me data for this book so that I can save time in locating relevant factual information. I believe that was when I had the most success, since I was using it to automate a specific task. Even then, I had to fix several erroneous citations later.

Finally, I have tried to use ChatGPT to create phrases to use during a tough conversation with a staff member, as was recommended by other administrators. I have also used it to create phrases to include in their evaluation. Once again, I found myself having to edit most of the language because I didn't like how generic it sounded. However, many of my colleagues swear by how helpful that was for them.

What Can School Leaders Do?

As promised in the introduction to this book, I aim to provide useful and practical recommendations to my fellow school leaders. This chapter described the challenge of never having enough time as a school leader. It might be tempting to simply ignore the discussion on AI altogether in favor of managing what appears urgent. However, I know that's not what you would want. The fact that you are reading this book should be an indication that you want to do something with AI. Below are some practical recommendations for a school leader who is not so sure about AI-enabled tools *yet*. These recommendations are exactly that, recommendations. However, they are certainly based on my experience:

Recommendation 1: Be open to learning and hearing about the latest AI-enabled tools and let your staff know of your stance explicitly.

As a leader, your explicit statement of priority allows your staff to engage you in a conversation. Once I openly shared my passion for learning technologies and interest in AI with staff, they came to me to let me know which tool they wanted to use or experiment with. Such collaboration became increasingly important as we learned more about the harm that biased AI models can inflict on our students and worked to protect them and our staff from potential harm.

Because I didn't make this crystal clear when ChatGPT and other AI-enabled tools would become available at my site earlier in the year, a staff member purchased several unauthorized AI Detection tools and used them to discipline one of her students. The situation became contentious when the parent challenged this classroom practice. Managing this experience spurred me to write the EdWeek Article, "No, AI Detection Won't Solve Cheating!" (Glazer, 2024) Since then, I have made it abundantly clear that no staff member should purchase an AI tool without first checking with site administration.

Recommendation 2: Go slow to go fast!

As much as you might feel pressured, you do not have to purchase an AI tool. In fact, it's better to go second than first when it comes to technology tools. This is coming from a technology lover.

If you read *The 74 Million*'s article "L.A. Schools Probe Charges its Hyped, Now-Defunct AI Chatbot Misused Student Data[21]" (Keierleber, 2024), you would understand why I suggest, "going slow to go fast" or, as one of my dear friends and colleagues, Ray Kimball, a retired Army Colonel, once told me, "Slow is smooth; smooth is fast." On July 10, 2024, *The 74 Million* broke the story on how the Los Angeles Unified School District (LAUSD)'s chatbot initiative had unwittingly exposed the data of its 540,000 students.

I remember watching LAUSD's Superintendent Alberto Carvalho speaking at an event hosted by Stanford, expressing his enthusiasm regarding individualized education of historically underserved students. While excited for the possibility, I was also concerned about the potential risk because my current district suffered from a ransomware attack in 2020, despite being located in the heart of Silicon Valley with so much access to an abundance of expertise on technology (Morgan, 2020)

---

[21] https://www.the74million.org/article/chatbot-los-angeles-whistleblower-allhere-ai/

General Recommendations for Administrators and Leaders

Use case and backward design considerations	Target users	Bias, discrimination, access:	Parental Consent:
What problem are we trying to solve?	○ Who will use the tool?	○ Request information on how the parent LLM and the tool has addressed bias and discrimination in the training data	○ If the parent LLM and/or the tool requires parental consent,
○ Who is using the tool?	○ What are the age restrictions of the LLM?		● How is parental consent collected/recorded?
● Teachers	○ How is privacy addressed?	○ Determine who would not benefit from the tool	● What are the plans for students whose families opt out of the tool use?
● Students	○ What information is shared with third parties? (This includes the parent LLM.)	○ Determine who would be unable to benefit from the tool	● Will opting out affect academic outcomes for the student? (Plans for those who opt out must be comparable to any using an AI tool.)
● Faculty/Staff	○ What are the guidelines for possible data breaches?		
○ Who benefits? Who is not included if using this tool?			

Figure 5: General Recommendations for Administrators and Leaders
(De Jesús, S & Glazer, K, 2024)

This is one reason why my colleague Sofía De Jesús and I wrote the *Framework for AI Implementation for Administrators and Leaders in K-12 Schools*[22], to ensure that school leaders ask good questions before purchasing any AI-enabled tools.

Recommendation 3: Leverage the on-campus expertise and teacher leaders.

One of the things that any great leader needs to constantly do is to build capacity and agency among the people they lead. Just as a teacher should always work to have their students become less dependent on them, I am a firm believer that the more opportunities you provide for your staff to become leaders, the better. Choosing and implementing AI-enabled tools on campus provides such a wonderful opportunity for you as a leader to leverage the on-campus expertise of your motivated teacher leaders.

For example, when we wanted to purchase BRISK, I asked several teachers to pilot it in their classrooms. Not only did my teachers, who piloted the program, provide me with great information about which tool to choose, but they also became supporters of the tools that we ultimately selected.

Recently, we had "Lunch and Learn," where one of our teachers hosted a workshop in his classroom during lunch so that he could demonstrate how he uses Google's NotebookLM with and for himself and his students. Other staff shared how helpful it was for them to see the way the tool was used in a real classroom context.

Recommendation 4: Build staff capacity by attending technology conferences.

When I was a classroom teacher, I wrote several grants in an effort to grow as a professional. I used the grant funds to attend various technology

---

[22] https://bit.ly/aiframeworkfork12leader

conferences, which solidified my desire to pursue my doctorate in learning technologies. I continued the practice when I became a school leader.

I highly recommend your staff in attending technology conferences such as ISTE, CUE, CoSN, or CITE. As you do, I also strongly suggest you encourage teachers to submit workshop proposals. Many of these conferences will provide scholarships or reduced registration fees for presenters. I also suggest you co-author a presentation. Such experiences will likely boost your staff's confidence and support their growth, as it did for me when I was a teacher. By offering to co-present, you also communicate how much you respect your teachers and their expertise.

Recommendation 5: Hire an outside expert as appropriate.

There is no way that a site leader can become an ultimate expert on AI, no matter how hard we try. In fact, I am highly suspicious of someone who claims to be one since the field is so rapidly changing. To expand our knowledge base, I invited an outside expert from Digital Promise when it was time for our District to learn about AI.

In January of 2024, a dear colleague of mine, Dr. Pati Ruiz from Digital Promise, delivered a keynote to our District staff members. As a nationally renowned expert in AI, she provided our staff with valuable insights and knowledge, enabling them to benefit from learning more about the research side of AI. Our staff still talks about that experience.

If you are looking for an organization with solid expertise and a focus on the public good, I suggest that you consider CSTA[23] and Digital Promise[24]. You can also find a list of organizations that are providing free workshops. If you are concerned about the budget for hiring an outside speaker, I recommend working with local universities or non-profit organizations funded by various grants, such as the NSF

---

[23] https://csteachers.org/
[24] https://digitalpromise.org/

or the US Department of Education grants, as many would have the requirements for dissemination.

Checklist for Leaders

- ✦ Establish a clear site-level policy for the adoption, vetting, and use of AI-enabled tools[25]
- ✦ Communicate the policy regularly to staff, students, and families through multiple channels (e.g., meetings, newsletters, training sessions)[26]
- ✦ Evaluate tools critically and holistically, considering pedagogical value, student privacy, equity implications, and long-term sustainability
- ✦ Form a site-based technology committee with diverse representation across grade levels, departments, and roles
- ✦ Task the committee with vetting new tools and ensuring alignment with instructional goals and district policies
- ✦ Pilot new tools with a small group of teacher leaders before scaling schoolwide implementation
- ✦ Build a shared repository of vetted lesson plans and instructional strategies that demonstrate best practices with the selected tool(s)
- ✦ Support teacher leaders in presenting their work at conferences by offering time, coaching, or funding when possible
- ✦ Elevate internal expertise by featuring teacher leaders during staff meetings, PD days, and cross-site learning opportunities
- ✦ Invite outside experts strategically to deepen staff understanding and bring fresh perspectives to your AI integration work

---

[25] Later in the book, I will share a tool that our students and I created that you can use to generate an editable policy.

[26] In Chapter 6, I will share three different ways that I worked with the students in creating such opportunities and what steps that we took to communicate the information to the community.

Ready to Lead Wrap Up

Leadership tension is an inevitable part of guiding a school community, especially as AI reshapes education in real time. Rather than resisting complexity, effective leaders acknowledge the gray areas and embrace the challenge of balancing competing demands. This chapter highlights how site leaders must juggle operational responsibilities with instructional vision, navigating evolving technologies, and managing diverse stakeholder expectations while supporting students and staff—which should be our primary focus at all times.

By leaning into this tension with intentional strategies, prioritizing communication, collaboration, and adaptability, you can transform uncertainty into purposeful action. Next, we turn our focus *upward*. We will explore how to build productive partnerships with the District Office. Understanding how to effectively manage up will empower you to influence policies and resources that directly impact your school's success with AI integration.

CHAPTER 2

⌒

Working with the District Office: Policy Clarity and Communication

"Leadership is a two-way street, loyalty up and loyalty down. Respect for one's superiors; care for one's crew."
–Admiral Grace Hopper, Inventor of the Compiler
and Recipient of the Medal of Freedom

Story from the Field: Choosing a Platform in a Hurry

In March 2020, at the start of the pandemic-related school closure, I attended a meeting with my superintendent, the entire executive cabinet, all the directors, and my fellow principals. There were over twenty principals in the district, and we were all participating in a meeting to make several key decisions. It was clear that we were going to do something drastic, like teaching all our students via an online conference platform. The next day, we were also brought together to evaluate an online platform for teacher training that would have cost the district close to $250,000.00. At the time, we were considering using the Elementary and Secondary School Emergency Relief (ESSER) funds to ensure that our students, staff, and families received instructional support.

During that meeting, I asked questions relating to pedagogy, various features of the platform, and how we would measure the usage data. I recall asking very specific questions about how the platform was built on the adult learning theory, only to get blank stares not only from the salesperson, but also from my colleagues. At some point in the meeting, one of the principals said, "We don't have time to listen to someone ask all these questions about this one platform. Can we just have the ETS[27] Director make these decisions? I want to know what the County guidance on COVID is this week."

That meeting crystallized my realization that I was not the instructional leader that I wished to be when I took the job as a high school principal.

The Distance Between the Ideal and the Reality

When I decided to become a principal, I wanted to do so because I was passionate about sharing my expertise and knowledge in learning technologies. To this day, I keep working on doing so—that's why I participated in various projects and webinars over the years. I am even writing this book because of it.

However, I was not doing much of that during my first year as principal. I was just trying to learn the job as the first-year principal when the pandemic hit. Even though I always had good intentions of becoming an instructional leader, the pandemic swiftly and thoroughly derailed those intentions. Instead of leading instructional initiatives

---

[27] ETS stands for Educational Technology Services. It was and still is a department in charge of all things technology at the Santa Barbara Unified School District.

during the school closure, my primary job became that of logistics coordinator and chief communicator.

Rather than thinking about and sharing the best online pedagogy to share with my teachers, I had to quickly learn how to run a webinar or to use a schoolwide messaging system, such as ParentSquare, to get the pertinent messages out to my school community. Rather than driving new and innovative instructional initiatives, I was creating flyers and videos so that I could share the most up-to-date information quickly and efficiently. I was buried under the pressure of managing the day-to-day, making numerous decisions regarding logistics, such as where to store thousands of masks or many gallons of hand sanitizer when we didn't have custodians on campus to do the work.

So my instructional leadership had to be offloaded to others on campus. I was extremely lucky to have a fantastic librarian, a skilled technology coach, and several content instructional coaches to support my teachers. But I yearned to be in the instructional space. After all, that was why I became a school leader: to influence teaching and learning, especially through the use of technology. Even though being a principal should have afforded me many opportunities to influence instructional decisions, I had very few occasions to do so during the pandemic.

For example, when we were getting ready to purchase an online teacher training tool, I provided feedback to the district leaders. In fact, I insisted on being present at every meeting, which was a challenge in and of itself because I had so many other meetings to attend, mostly hearing about the federal, state, and county updates on COVID. Still, I persisted.

Just before the final decision to purchase a teacher online training platform was made, I shared with my district leaders that the tool was unlikely to be used by my teachers, because I had identified several issues with the user interface. I raised numerous concerns regarding the unfriendly user interface for adult learners. The answer, unfortunately, was that there was nothing better out there, and we had to use the funds or we would lose them completely if we didn't spend them. So I said if we had to purchase it, at least we should ask for the features that we want. After all, we are the paying customers, and they should deliver the product that we can use.

Because I continued to raise objections, the vendor requested a meeting with me to discuss the issues. During that meeting, I made it clear to the vendor that I was not trying to derail their sale. I told them that I was simply doing my job as a good steward of public funds. I shared my background in learning science and asked them to consider adding features based on learning science and adult learning principles. I argued that the current organization of the information didn't invite positive experiences or interactions from my teachers. I told them that something good needs to happen after a maximum of three clicks[28]. I also suggested creating a user interface that was more like a "choose your own adventure" with large buttons rather than the tiny text that their platform had. I made several other suggestions during that meeting. Of course, none of that was incorporated, and the District moved forward with the platform. I knew that would happen eventually no matter what I did, but I felt I had to try. In the end, I was not surprised that only a handful of my teachers used a fraction of the training module. The use rate was less than 2% when the contract ended.

When the 2021-2022 school year began, I continued to encounter situations where I attempted to contribute with my background knowledge. Unfortunately, it was extremely limited due to the demands of my job as a site leader who had to keep our students and staff safe on campus. To be fair, my district leaders encouraged me to participate whenever they could; however, the amount of work that I had to get done to stay afloat as we were attempting to bring our students and staff back to campus didn't leave me much time to focus on teaching and learning.

---

[28] I call this the "three-click" rule. No matter how good the information is, if a teacher has to click more than three or four times to get to it, they will quit. The only time they don't is if they were the one who created the materials.

That experience made me question what I, as a site leader, can do to balance the needs between the operational and instructional demands of a school site. When I moved to Mountain View in July of 2022, I was hopeful that I might finally be able to use my background and knowledge to influence teaching and learning on our campus. I even participated in a series of listening sessions on AI hosted by the US Department of Education and served as a panelist for the webinar launching the document, "Artificial Intelligence and the Future of Teaching and Learning," on July 6, 2023.

Just as the Global Pandemic forced me to become more of a bureaucrat than the instructional leader I wanted to be, the recent proliferation of GenAI in schools is forcing me to be more of a policy enforcer than an instructional leader. But I am using the learning that I have gained during the pandemic to remediate my current situation. I would be lying if I said I have figured out how to do that perfectly. I do feel, however, that I am closer to achieving that goal now that I have spent some time considering and implementing a few specific strategies, and I sincerely hope that my recommendations will resonate with other principals, whose desire is to become instructional leaders. I also hope that aspiring administrators or even teachers will find these useful so they can understand what their site leaders might be experiencing.

Working with the District Office

As a site leader, I am a middle manager. I am the intermediary between district leaders and site personnel. The biggest challenge of being a middle manager is balancing the demands from my superiors, including School Board Members, Superintendent, Executive Cabinet members, and the District Office staff, with the demands from my staff.

For the most part, everyone's needs should be aligned in terms of each party's desire to support students. But at times, each party's needs can diverge based on the information that they have access to and what they are ultimately responsible for. Just as I thought my primary job was instructional leadership, but ended up spending more time on logistics, many entities that believe they are acting in the best interest of students can see things vastly differently.

In the case of AI implementation, there is an added issue: the lack of technical knowledge about the tools themselves, and how these tools influence the school ecosystem as a whole while they simultaneously cause societal changes.

Who's in Charge?

Parents and staff alike are sometimes very surprised to find out that education is governed by each state in the United States, which means that what is legal in Massachusetts or Florida may not be in California. To make the matter complicated, there are several other laws and regulations impacting schools that derive from federal and local agencies.

For example, you might have heard of Title IX. As a site principal, I had to conduct many investigations relating to this federal regulation that states, "Title IX protects people from discrimination based on sex in education programs or activities that receive federal financial assistance" (U.S. Department of Education, 2025)

As a site administrator, I also need to be familiar with the District's Board Policies (BP) and the Administrative Regulations (AR) that are designed to direct the work of the site administrators. Finally, a site principal is supposed to set the site policies based on the BP and the AR that are supposed to be practical applications of the State Education Code and Federal Regulations.

As much as the general public believes that a site principal is "in charge" of a school, there really are a lot of layers of bureaucracy that a site leader must contend with in addition to working with the school community. As a result, it takes time for a school to quickly respond when it comes to fast-changing technology such as AI.

Whose Timeline?

In addition to understanding the different regulations that govern a school site, a site leader must be aware of timelines that exist beyond the school site. For example, the US Department of Education published "Artificial Intelligence and the Future of Teaching and Learning[29]" in March of 2023. Since then, the State of California has published its guidance of "Learning With AI, Learning About AI: Information regarding the role of artificial intelligence (AI) in California K12 education[30]" (California Department of Education, 2025), which included a resource kit[31].

As you can see from the timeline above, it took nearly a year for the State of California to create guidance on AI after the federal government acted. Utah was the first state that created a guiding document on GenAI about a month prior to California in March of 2024 (Levi, Ridgway, Simon, Slawe, & Oh, 2024). As of September of 2024, there are still several states that have not officially adopted any guidance[32]. This meant that our school board was not necessarily in a rush to create guidance on AI. In fact, our current district office does not have a comprehensive policy on AI as yet.

Setting Your Own Pace

Having been a high school principal for a few years through the pandemic and beyond, I learned a few valuable lessons in terms of an implementation timeline. As a site leader, I have the responsibility of

---

[29] https://www.ed.gov/sites/ed/files/documents/ai-report/ai-report.pdf

[30] https://www.cde.ca.gov/ci/pl/aiincalifornia.asp

[31] https://www.cde.ca.gov/ci/pl/documents/cdeairesourcekit.pdf

[32] According to the National Conference of State Legislators, "In the 2023 legislative session, at least 25 states, Puerto Rico and the District of Columbia introduced artificial intelligence bills, and 18 states and Puerto Rico adopted resolutions or enacted legislation" (NCSL, 2024).

tending to our immediate staff and families when it comes to executing a district policy. It is definitely important for site leaders to implement and execute the policy of the district; however, I no longer simply accept the new district policy as a mandate for immediate implementation. I learned to voice my concerns, if there were any, to help leaders be thoughtful and deliberate. I also learned to push district leaders to expedite certain items when I see a compelling need at our school. Because I interact with our staff, students, and families on a daily basis, I am able to gauge what I call "the temperament and the tempo" of my own school community.

In fact, I believe it is my responsibility to inform district leaders so they understand the needs of my immediate school community. As the person on the front line, I am able to care for my superiors by sharing what I observe to be my site's priority based on the information I receive from staff, students, and families.

What Can Site Leaders Do?

I believe AI implementation is no different from any other initiative site leaders want to implement. To do so effectively, I recommend the following when working with the district:

Recommendation 1: Become familiar with the Acceptable Usage Policy (AUP) and other existing technology-related policies

When it comes to AI-enabled tools adoption, a site leader must be well-versed in the AUP and tech policies that govern all types of technology tools. Because the actual administration of the policies and disciplinary actions when there is a policy violation typically occur at the site level, it's important that site leaders are well-versed in these types of policies.

Recommendation 2: Be mindful of the available tech training calendar

Whether it is an AI tool or any tech tool, ongoing training is key to successful implementation. Check to see if there is a tech training calendar so you can set your own site's training calendar. If there is none, make a recommendation to the District Office to create one so that the training becomes the norm, not the exception.

Recommendation 3: Become aware of the district's urgent priorities

I have seen site leaders who aren't necessarily aware of their district's priority. For example, your district leaders might not want to make a drastic policy movement during an election year with the potential for getting a whole new school board. Or the district may now have unexpected budgetary constraints. Understanding the district's priorities can assist a site leader in determining which agenda items should be prioritized at the site level.

Recommendation 4: Pay attention to the calendars that govern the District's operations

Similarly, the District office maintains a calendar based on state mandates, reporting deadlines, and data release timelines. Just as the site activities are influenced by various school calendars and athletic seasons, district operations are likely to be influenced by their own calendars. Becoming aware of them can help site leaders become much more effective in advancing their agendas.

Recommendation 5: Develop a close relationship with the District's technology department in all aspects

It's important to build a strong working relationship with the Instructional Technology (IT) Department because school operations require constant interaction with the technology department. To think of IT as a separate entity that handles something outside of core instruction is no longer possible in today's school leadership. Disciplining a student or investigating a theft on campus often requires the cooperation of the technology department. If you work for a small district that doesn't have a department, work with the individual in charge of your school's technology to implement the best practices.

In particular, you should always be aware of IT infrastructure development, including the WiFi access on campus. I still remember having a conversation with my Director of Technology about the lack of WiFi access in our school's front parking lot and on the baseball field. Because we had many conversations about the infrastructure, I was able to convince him of our site's needs.

Recommendation 6: Be an active partner with the IT department

Organizations such as California IT in Education[33] (CITE) or Consortium for School Networking[34] (CoSn) have published AI guidance for IT professionals that is useful. The International Society for Technology in Education[35] (ISTE) has also published general guidance for school districts. I recommend that you, as a site leader, become an active partner in what is being introduced to your school's ecosystem.

---

[33] https://www.cite.org/ai-resources
[34] https://www.cosn.org/ai/
[35] https://iste.org/ai

Remember: as a site leader you are ultimately the one to answer questions from staff, students, and families when it comes to what happens on your site. It pays to be an active partner in the selection and implementation of any tool that is on your campus.

Checklist for Leaders

- Review and understand the district's Acceptable Use Policy (AUP) and related technology usage guidelines
- Familiarize yourself with existing Board Policies (BP) and Administrative Regulations (AR) related to AI, data privacy, and digital tools.
- Stay informed about the full range of tech tools available to your staff, including any that are AI-enabled or under consideration
- Review your School Board's stated goals and priorities to assess whether AI and instructional technology are strategic focus areas
- Monitor the district's IT infrastructure investments, ensuring your site has reliable WiFi, power, and hardware to support AI-enabled tools
- Advocate for and participate in ongoing technology training for all staff to build collective capacity and confidence
- Recommend the creation of a district-level tech committee, or if one exists, ensure your site is represented to voice local needs and contexts

Ready to Lead Wrap Up

The experience of working with district leaders through the chaos of a pandemic and into the unpredictable terrain of GenAI has taught me a powerful lesson: the site principal must be both *a listener and a translator*. You must hear the hopes and constraints from above, and echo the aspirations and realities from below. In this delicate balance lies the true art of leadership, not just managing up, but leading across both vertically and horizontally. If AI is going to be more than another initiative, site leaders must be *trusted agents of coherence*.

> If AI is going to be more than another initiative, site leaders must be *trusted agents of coherence*.

In the next chapter, we'll turn the lens inward, focusing on how to lead your staff through the complexity of adopting AI tools in their classrooms. From assessing readiness to creating a comprehensive professional development plan, we'll explore how to lead with clarity, courage, and care.

CHAPTER 3

～

Working with Your Teaching Staff: Building Trust and Competence

"Collecting a teacher's knowledge may help us solve the challenges of the day, but understanding how a teacher thinks can help us navigate the challenges of a lifetime."
–Adam Grant, American organizational psychologist and author

Story from the Field: An Unexpected Purchase Request

Imagine you are a site leader, and you get an email from a staff member requesting that you purchase a tech tool. If you are lucky, that staff member hasn't yet used it with students. More often than not, however, you are likely to learn that a teacher has already used the tool with their students after being offered a free introductory subscription. In some cases, you never even find out because they have chosen to pay for the subscription themselves.

I have encountered a situation where not only has a teacher been using a tool without authorization, but they have also requested funds from crowdfunding sites to continue a particular subscription. Sometimes, a district has a strong IT department that will prevent the use of unauthorized tools on campus by setting up a filter. Undaunted or even sometimes emboldened by such a preventative measure, a teacher may use a personal hotspot to circumvent the filters. At a district such as ours, where we allow students to bring their own devices to class, such issues can be compounded as students might also use their own personal hotspots to access content that should be filtered.

Teachers Going "Rogue"

If you have been a classroom teacher, you might be familiar with the following scenario: You attend a tech conference, read a tech blog, or even see a social media post and become aware of a new tech tool that many educators are raving about. So you decide to try it for yourself. After signing up for a free version, you realize that a truly useful part of the tool is behind a paywall or is only available when you pay for a subscription. At this point, you have a choice to make.

When I was a teacher working in a district that heavily relied on Title I funds, I knew that my yearly department supply budget was about $200 a year, and I had to make it last for the markers, papers, pencils, or notebooks my students needed for the year. Considering my classroom budget situation, I never thought I could ask my department chair or my administrator to provide additional funds for me to purchase tech tools. Instead, I would work directly with a technology company as a classroom teacher so I could try these tools for free. I was very lucky that I knew enough to let my IT team know that I was using these free tools for my classroom when I chose a learning management system (LMS) for one school year. Before my district adopted an authorized LMS, I was able to become familiar with the general structure of an

LMS so that I was prepared to use a variety of features when an official one was launched.

I find myself relying on that learning experience when I am asked to use an LMS. Recently, I was asked to teach a class for aspiring administrators where I was required to use an LMS that I was not too familiar with. But remembering the fundamentals of most LMS certainly helped me not to have to spend hours learning how to become familiar with the platform.

Avoiding the Pitfalls

Unfortunately, when it comes to instructional technologies with or without AI, teachers can be unwittingly left to their own devices. This can lead to potentially catastrophic situations. For example, I remember visiting the Massachusetts Institute of Technology Media Lab in 2014 where a researcher asked the visiting adult students in a doctoral program to provide him with their personal email accounts to demonstrate the speed and the effectiveness of a social mapping tool that he was developing. When my fellow doctoral student did just that, he used her personal email address to create a social network map (similar to the graphic below) of all of her personal correspondences with a single click.

He boasted that he was able to run the analysis to see if she had broken up with her boyfriend or not. I remember asking him about how he was drawing such conclusions and what the error rate was. Eventually, he said that he needed millions of such emails to draw any useful conclusions. I later learned that the tool was able to use lots of email addresses because signing up for a free email account automatically granted the company access to the email data. Even back in 2014, these types of technologies were being used to collect personal data that was later commercialized and to train various AI models. If this was happening back then, imagine what is possible now!

Figure 6: Gephi network visualization (Martin, 2014)

Seeing that demonstration and learning about what was behind the tool made me realize why so many companies were interested in being in schools. According to an EdWeek Article, tech companies want to be in the PreK-12 space because of the brand loyalty they get from the students using their tool or platform earlier in their lives. These tech companies are cultivating lifelong customers (Klein, 2020). In addition, they also get massive amounts of data from being in the school system that can not only reveal the pattern but also influence behaviors.

For example, in July of 2025, the American Federation of Teachers and the United Federation of Teachers entered into an agreement with companies such as Microsoft, OpenAI, and Anthropic to receive free AI training and curriculum. These companies are investing 23 million dollars into building the National Academy for AI Instruction to gain access to the data generated by their 1.8 million teacher members

(AFT, 2025). While this move may bring a significant benefit to these organizations, the tradeoff would be giving these organizations access to data of millions of teachers and, by extension, their students.

What Teachers Want–from a Principal's Perspective

When I ask my educator colleagues, they universally express a similar desire when it comes to AI-enabled tools. Educators want AI-enabled tools that are easy to use and helpful to their students. They want tools that are effective for student engagement and learning. Because many LLMs are considered to have been biased and have caused harm to certain groups[36], many educators I have met recently, including teachers at my current school site, are genuinely concerned about using AI-enabled tools with their students. They are concerned about unwittingly exposing their students to harm and themselves to legal liabilities.

I believe educators are also frankly tired of the conversations under the guise of improving education that are essentially about replacing teachers because they recognize this to be truly about reducing labor costs, not about improving student learning. It is no surprise that the United Kingdom is reported to be the first country to debut a teacherless classroom[37]. Such a movement towards a dystopian future of education is what turns teachers against AI.

One thing that I definitely learned from the pandemic is how much we need to realize the importance of our schools. Education is more than cramming discrete pieces of information into our students' brains quicker and faster using AI. It truly is a society's effort to create an

---

[36] In 2024, NAACP published a brief regarding the AI used and its potential harm towards racial profiling.

[37] "From September 2024, David Game College will be piloting an alternative programme of study for GCSE students - the first of its kind in the UK - with all core subjects being taught entirely by AI-driven adaptive learning platforms," the school says on its website.

educated populace in the protection of democracy. By interacting with peers and overcoming challenges, students become independent adults, and schoolhouse experiences that facilitate such life experiences are crucial to education.

What Can Leaders Do?

As a site administrator, I consider my primary job to be akin to a stagehand or a theater manager. My job is to construct the most impactful stage so that my stars (a.k.a. my teachers) can do their job of being effective with their students. In other words, I constantly think about how to remove their barriers and to resource my teachers effectively so that they can do their job best. To that end, a site leader can do a lot for their staff.

Recommendation 1: Reassure your teachers of their current importance in the educational ecosystem

I summarily reject the notion that AI can ever replace teachers, and I have been vocal in defending my fellow educators. That's not to say that I think that AI won't impact education. It certainly will. However, I firmly believe that our students must be educated by well-trained teachers who can leverage all useful technology tools, in particular AI-enabled and AI-supported tech tools. Continue to reassure your teachers that you currently lead by making your support and advocacy as explicit as possible.

Recommendation 2: Focus the conversation on sound pedagogy beyond individual tools

As you continue to assure your teachers of their importance, you should also encourage them to continuously improve their pedagogical skills. I know that many teachers want practical solutions. I remember submitting a few proposals in 2016 to the ISTE Conference and getting accepted on my first try, which I have been told is unlikely to happen. I learned from that experience. A proposal built on a specific platform is more likely to be chosen and have a lot more attendees. As much as I understand why that might happen, I realize the need to focus on strong pedagogy when it comes to technology tools, because many of the tools featured in the previous year's conference were no longer available the following year.

Even a highly popular tool can be discontinued—such as the discontinuance of Flipgrid in October 2024[38]. Tech tools will come and go, regardless of the number of users it has at any given moment. In fact, it is inevitable for a tech tool to become obsolete at some point or undergo drastic changes in features. I think of this as something like a car. It does matter to a certain degree which maker and model of a car you drive. Certainly, who is driving also matters. But ultimately, a car's purpose is to *transport people and goods*, which is why it has tires, big or small, so that it can move from one place to another. Whether a car has a backup camera or an automatic lock, if it can't do its primary function of supporting movement, it would be useless. Likewise, any educational technology tool that can't enhance sound pedagogy is of little value. Educators need to develop instruction that is tool-agnostic.

To cultivate such a mindset, principals need to encourage teachers to adopt sound pedagogical strategies, including competency-based learning, collaborative learning, reciprocal teaching, and inquiry-based instruction, among others. Doing so will also empower teachers to use their skills as professionals, regardless of the tools available to them.

In the hands of a skilled instructor, even paper and pencil can become the most powerful piece of technology. You don't need to have AI-enabled tools to be an incredible teacher. In fact, if there is no sound pedagogy, introducing additional tech can make things worse in a classroom. As

---

[38] This has created a widespread panic among many educators, and #RIPFlipgrid trending on various social media platforms for weeks.

technology tools become more sophisticated, teachers need to strengthen their pedagogical skills to take charge of the learning environment, and a school leader must be able to support them in this endeavor.

Recommendation 3: Provide use cases specific to the developmental stages or the contents

Focusing on pedagogy doesn't mean ignoring the needs of staff to see a specific use case. Just as a great piece of writing comes alive with specific examples, providing a specific use case can reinforce strong pedagogical practices in the classroom.

When doing so, I recommend that you consider students' developmental stages. First, any student under thirteen is not allowed to use any GenAI tools in many states, including the State of California. Second, you want to equip staff to feel confident in helping their students gain AI literacy.

Below is the second table included in the document[39] that my friend Sofía De Jesús and I created as a part of our year-long project for the CSTA Equity Fellowship Project. Our goal was to provide practical recommendations to K-12 school leaders for the new AI-enabled tools. We grounded our recommendations on several documents that were published by reputable organizations, and we wanted to ensure that school leaders were able to support their staff at various grade levels.

Recommendation 4: Inform your teachers of the district's policy regarding AI-enabled tools use and guard against the temptation for free tools

Because a school district collects a lot of information from its students and families, it is important that school leaders are well-versed in the

---

[39] The document is called, "Framework for Administrators and Decision-makers on AI Implementation in Schools."

Grade Level Sample Recommendations for Teachers

K-2	3-5	6-8	9-12
• Identify technology around you.	• Identify and discuss the differences between a chatbot and a search engine	• Model reading Terms of Service, Terms of Use, and Privacy Policies of the tools we interact with every day	• Explore the legal consequences of privacy and intellectual property laws (limitations and safeguards, for example)
• Explain how we interact with technology (TVs, computers, phones, tablets) appropriately in simple terms.	• Define bias and discrimination and how they can creep into the technology we are using	• Explore ways that privacy may be violated by the tools used in everyday life, including at school and at home	• Explore and discuss how some biases built into the training data can affect different communities differently
• Help the students understand how watching one show (or seeing an social media post) is used to recommend other shows by pointing out the use of advertisement or encouragements.	• Explain how training data is used to create AI and GenAI tools	• Explain how technology tools can be used to violate one's privacy and what students can do to stop that practice	• Discuss, evaluate, challenge, and analyze the Terms of Service, Terms of Use, and Privacy Policies and recommend changes to help safeguard the users.
• Actively safe online searches and encourage the students enlist teacher or parent when doing so.	• Explore and discuss how historical data can contain bias and how that bias can affect many aspects of life (health, legal entertainment, and more).	• Discuss how AI and GenAI can affect our perceptions of a topic, such as when algorithms affect what information we are presented	• Explain and discuss the social implications of using chatbots, tutors, and other GenAI (exploring how outputs can all be similar given similar prompts, effects on originality, and more)
• Explain how screen-time may impact all aspects of their lives	• Learn about, explore, discuss, and challenge use of copyrighted texts, images, and videos	• Demonstrate the errors (a.k.a. hallucinations) and discuss potential issues with incorrect information	
• Have discussions about having an online presence and how to talk to others online, when is it safe, and how to keep information private	• Identify ways, both positive and negative, that AI and GenAI can impact accessibility	• Explain why anthropomorphizing AI and using terms such as "hallucination" is harmful to everyone	

Figure 7 - Grade Level Sample Recommendations for Teachers
(De Jesús, S & Glazer, K, 2024)

privacy policies of the state. In general, teachers do not want to break rules, and I consider protecting their academic freedom to be a part of a school leader's job.

As we continue to bring more AI-enabled tools to our school's ecosystem, school leaders must ensure that staff members are well-informed and supported. To do so, a leader must become well-versed in which AI-enabled tools are purchased or allowed to be used in the district. I would also strongly encourage schools to avoid using free tools unless it is explicitly stated that they are not collecting student data in exchange for the free services.

When it comes to technology tools, there really is no free lunch, and your data is being collected even if you are paying for the use. When you use free tools in schools, the price is more than likely access to student data, and I believe that it would be unethical to summarily make the decision for your students without providing them the option to opt out.

Recommendation 5: Model the judicious implementation of all education technology tools, including AI-enabled tools

When ChatGPT was first released, I definitely tried it to see how useful it would be. Though the tool has improved considerably in terms of accuracy, I don't see it saving a lot of time. In fact, I believe that it might take longer for an expert to use GenAI tools to create high-quality products. For example, I used ChatGPT to write an evaluation for one staff member, which was considered a recommended use case for a school leader. ChatGPT produced a ton of texts, but the sentences were so generic that I ended up rewriting the whole thing, which took me much longer than if I had done it all on my own.

It is possible that I need to get better at prompt engineering to get the results that I need from these tools. Still, I believe that we need to critically examine the notion of faster and more always being better. I think of that as a possible difference between a buffet restaurant versus eating at home. You might be able to eat a lot of food at a buffet restaurant at a lower price, but the food may not taste as good or as nutritious as the food that you can get at home, especially if you are cooking with love and care.

Furthermore, the promise of instructional technology transforming education has yet to be actualized. In fact, U.S. schools have yet to bridge the access and achievement gaps, even with all the investment (Kucirkova, 2024). Therefore, school leaders should model judicious implementation of education technology tools to improve student learning and instruction rather than buy into the hype.

Checklist for Leaders

- Tend to teachers' concerns regarding students cheating by working with staff to reexamine and/or reestablish academic honesty policies
- Educate teachers of the harm that can come from using cheating detection tools
- Redirect the conversation to developing teachers' pedagogical skills
- Work with teachers to vet and evaluate AI-enabled tools to improve student learning
- Highlight the best pedagogical practices using AI-enabled tools
- Work with district leadership to provide clear guidance on AI tool use for instruction
- Provide training opportunities for staff to become familiar with a variety of AI-enabled tools to build AI literacy among teachers
- Model the use of AI tools and other technology so that staff can learn to rely on the leaders

Ready to Lead Wrap Up

I do not believe site leaders need to be the most tech-savvy person in the room. However, when it comes to AI-enabled tools at schools, leaders need to become fully willing to model appropriate use. Site leaders need to be the leaders who are willing: willing to learn with teachers, willing to listen to their concerns, and willing to make a decision to provide what they need.

A site leader should be the person who provides resources for teachers and removes unnecessary barriers to teacher effectiveness and student learning. That core responsibility has not changed because of AI. Teachers are not resisting AI because they are afraid of innovation; they are resisting because they fear being erased from the process, from decision-making, and from the classroom (Guerra-López, 2025). As leaders, our job is to ensure that does not happen, and also to communicate our firm commitment to preserving the humanity of our educators.

The good news? According to the EdWeek article, teachers and students alike are asking for exactly that (Langreo, 2025). They need policies that protect them, training that empowers them, and leaders who walk the talk. When you build systems that center instructional purpose and ethical care, you can transform fear into curiosity and resistance into readiness.

> When you build systems that center instructional purpose and ethical care, you can transform fear into curiosity and resistance into readiness.

In the next chapter, we'll shift our focus to the often-overlooked backbone of our schools: our support staff. From office clerks and custodians to paraprofessionals and cafeteria staff, these essential team members play a crucial role in creating a safe, inclusive, and technology-enabled learning environment. We'll explore how to ensure they are informed, trained, and valued as part of your school's AI transition.

CHAPTER 4

Working with Extended Staff: Inclusivity Across All Roles

"Great things in business are never done by one person.
They're done by a team of people."
—Steve Jobs, American businessman, inventor,
and co-founder of Apple

Story from the Field: The Forgotten Group

When I became an assistant principal overseeing athletics and activities, I learned very quickly how much time is wasted on repetitive and clerical tasks. Unfortunately, there aren't many school-appropriate tools that are designed to fit the school ecosystem. Furthermore, there isn't enough investment to develop such tools. For example, there is only one program that a school can use for managing Associated Student Body finance that I know of in the State of California, because companies do not necessarily want to be in the market with such a small profit margin. The yearbook market is a tiny bit better, with a few companies from which to choose.

Because of the lack of options in tools that meet complicated compliance mandates, many schools try to make do with tools that are designed for other industries. To make matters worse, many school systems do not invest in training of the support staff for tech tools that are in use. If one of the benefits of bringing AI tools into schools is to improve efficiency in teaching and learning, shouldn't we also consider making things more efficient for our staff who manage the bureaucratic demands of running a school?

Any educator who has worked at a school knows that two groups of people you never want to upset are the principal's assistant—or any administrative assistants in the office, for that matter—and the custodians. If you are on their list for whatever reason, your life will be absolutely miserable.

Yet, rarely does a school system provide professional learning for these important support staff members, even though they are the ones who make the operations of the school possible by keeping the facilities safe and clean, purchasing and distributing textbooks and classroom supplies, keeping track of attendance, processing payroll, and providing breakfast and lunch to the students. Sadly, many administrators are former teachers who lack training on the operations of the school. Even though I took classes on school finance, the accounting knowledge that I have originated from taking three accounting classes prior to my education training. Similarly, all my knowledge of technology is largely self-taught or came from my studies toward my doctorate in learning technologies.

Working with Support Staff as a Technology Coach

When I became the Instructional Technology Coach for a large District, my primary job was to support classroom teachers. While supporting the teachers, I realized that providing technology training devoid of pedagogical support was ineffective. I also learned that I had to meet the teachers where they were, and many teachers really wanted another human to show them how to do things, even though they were absolutely capable of learning things by watching YouTube videos. In fact, they would openly say that they know they could watch the videos, but they would rather I spent time with them. That experience taught me the importance of collaborative learning for adults.

In addition, it was not the lack of tools that was the problem. In fact, many office staff had more tools than they knew what to do with. Seeing this, I decided to take a different approach to my training for the support staff. On one occasion, I spent half a day with an administrative assistant who was trying to manage all the requests to use the school facilities. She needed a tool that would streamline the process, from a request to use a location on campus, to the approval of the use, to generating the setup request for custodians. Essentially, she was requesting a way to manage the entire workflow that was specific to her school. I ended up setting up a Google Site with several Google Calendars. I worked on a Google Form that could generate a PDF file of the request because the head custodian preferred a paper copy that he could write on as he was asking his crew to set up, which made sense because the school was not going to issue a tablet or a smartphone to its custodial crew. When I checked back in a few weeks, I received positive feedback from everyone involved. In particular, the head custodian was thankful that his recommendations were accepted even though he didn't typically like using technology.

Supporting Non-Teaching Support Staff

As much as a school exists to educate, we can't do so without all our support staff members. Leaders must recognize that and invest in the support staff. Decisions should be made in terms of who is using what tools to complete their tasks efficiently. For instance, if you are purchasing new computers or monitors, leaders should remember the front office staff members who spend more time staring at a computer screen longer than a teacher would. What about a campus safety staff member who needs access to a campus map or student photos? Do they need a tablet, too? These considerations made to the support staff can improve student and staff experiences drastically and should not be ignored.

Lack of or Uneven Technology Skills among Support Staff

Because teachers are generally required to have a bachelor's degree at a minimum, we can generally assume that teachers know how to use some basic tech tools. Since the pandemic, tech proficiency among teachers has also improved drastically. Also, schools are very used to providing technology training for teachers. So teachers have opportunities to gain tech skills, even if those opportunities are limited.

However, the same can't be said about support staff. They are often left out or thought of as an extension of the teaching staff. They also tend to perform specific tasks that require specialized training in technology. For example, our textbook clerk uses one platform, a combination of textbook inventory tracking and fee tracking for lost books, while the registrar uses a completely different platform to manage student information. The registrar also has to use another platform that connects our school with various universities, both domestic and international, since he has to send transcripts to them. Unfortunately, he is the only one who uses it as the feature is specific to his role. And our attendance clerk manages our phone system, Student Information System (SIS), and also regularly runs reports to be shared with the administration so that we can follow up with truant students. All of these tasks are vital and require a level of technical skill, yet they rarely receive attention, let alone training.

Opportunities Afforded by AI

When we consider all the benefits of AI, we often consider improving productivity by reducing repetitive and mundane tasks. Yet, when we discuss educational technology, school leaders—by extension, classroom teachers or even technology companies—don't always appear to consider support staff.

I frequently receive advertisements about AI-enabled tools for schools. Many of them, however, don't quite fit or address the needs of our support staff. Even when they claim that the tools are for schools, many tools are designed for businesses, not educational institutions. A tool that is being used for schools needs to have specific safeguards that are specific to each state. Many schools also have different needs based on demographics, community context, or even just their size[40]. Over the years, I have worked with many education technology companies that build tools and promise modifications to fit site-specific needs. Unfortunately, that rarely materializes, which leads to many tools being unused or underused[41].

When fairly well-designed tools are introduced or purchased, it is often up to the individual school and its staff members to figure out how they might fit into the specific school ecosystem. Such a reality creates a level of frustration that often leads to implementation failure (Johnson et. al., 2016). For support staff, such a technology implementation cliff is much more acute because they are often neglected by the primary decision-makers at the site, such as their site principal whose primary focus is the classroom teacher.

---

[40] According to California Department of Education (CDE) enrollment data (2023–24), school sizes in the state range from fewer than 30 students in small rural K–8 schools to more than 5,000 in large urban high schools (DataQuest; NCES Common Core of Data). CDE also reports that the percentage of English Language learners can vary from 1% to 80% (CDE, 2024).

[41] According to the Associated Press article, "Schools' pandemic spending boosted tech companies. Did it help US students?", US Congress provided $190 billion dollars to schools during the pandemic with few reporting requirements (Binkley, 2023).

Please don't misunderstand me. I am not "blaming" principals. I am just acknowledging that we must put extra effort into supporting our support staff if we want it to happen. When you have to manage hundreds of certified and support staff, it is almost inevitable that some things will be overlooked. However, we cannot overlook our support staff team members when it comes to technology and technology training. If you are offering training for Google Workspace, why not offer specific training on Google Forms or Google Sheets to the clerical staff members?

How can we use AI to improve the operational functions of a high school? Recently, our Athletic Director (AD) told me that a group of ADs asked ChatGPT to create a schedule for games because they had to add a new sport into an already crowded game schedule. According to him, they were very impressed by the result; however, the League Commissioner[42] declined to use the schedule. Instead, he chose to create the schedule by hand. I asked my AD if the final schedule that ChatGPT created was inaccurate or problematic. He stated that it was no worse than the human-created schedule because of so many constraints that it had to consider. He said that the human-created one was slightly better because he knew the fields a bit better, and he knew the traffic patterns. He felt that if the ADs had the information that the Commissioner had, they could have easily added additional constraints or information to improve the outcome, which is the very definition of what an AI can do.

Practical Challenges of Working with Support Staff

If you have ever worked in a school system, you know that having the office staff on your side can make your life easier. In fact, I have been

---

[42] This is the person who adjudicates the rules of the athletic league consisting of a number of high schools within a specific area. This person has the authority to approve or deny requests from member schools.

told by a number of administrators to be nice to the support staff, because they typically have the power to make or break administrators who might have the titles, but not the influence, necessary to impact an organization. Because of that, I have seen school leaders who don't necessarily ask the right questions.

For example, I have no idea how many words a minute my assistant can type to this date. I don't even know that she knows that information herself. I recently discovered that she only has limited knowledge of spreadsheets, including the use of basic functions such as sum or copy cells. She did not know how to use more complex formulas that could potentially help her complete her tasks much more efficiently. Because I assumed that she knew how to do the formulas and set up a spreadsheet to use them, I didn't provide her with detailed instructions. I realized many weeks later that the spreadsheet was incorrectly updated because she accidentally deleted a formula that I added to a cell.

This posed an interesting challenge. Clearly, I knew that teaching her how to use the formulas would be best for everyone; however, I barely had the time to set up the sheet to get the work done, let alone the time to teach her all the details. I thought about asking the district trainer to come and teach her what I needed her to know; however, that still required me–or someone–to spend time with both of them to show exactly what I needed to be done because the spreadsheet was addressing a specific need that I had. Rather than going down that path, I ended up deciding to lock particular tabs and color-code specific cells, so she knew precisely where her cells began and mine ended. I felt that the solution actually worked for us, because she is highly competent in accurate record-keeping.

After becoming an administrator, I had to spend more time working with our support staff as their manager and supervisor. I realized there are two distinct issues that a leader must urgently address when it comes to working with the support staff. First, I believe that the sense of agency and self-worth has eroded considerably among our support staff since the pandemic. Yet, there isn't a lot of research being done to measure such despair or what needs to be done to improve it if, indeed, such a phenomenon exists. In fact, I am only speaking of this based on the conversations that I have had with my own staff, who interact with me on a daily basis since becoming an administrator, a sample size of no more than twenty.

For example, my previous assistant left the profession altogether, citing the increased stress. Considering how she and I weathered the pandemic together and how strong she was all along, it surprised me when she told me she was leaving not only the position but also the education field. When I asked what had prompted her to make that decision, she said that she had stayed in her job because I was her supervisor and she felt a personal connection to me. After I left the school, she lost that sense of connection with her new principal, so she decided to leave the education field altogether. According to the Rand 2022 study, during the COVID-era and beyond, U.S. teachers and principals are experiencing stress and burnout at about twice the rate of other working adults, which threatens both educator well-being and the quality of student learning.

Based on recent reports of educators who feel demoralized and overwhelmed to an unprecedented level (Chambers, 2025), it is not difficult to imagine that support staff feel the same level of stress, due to the high level of school absenteeism data, not only among students but also staff (Blad, 2023).

Second, what used to be simpler secretarial duties at school are no longer simple. The front office staff now must have a level of technological skills with all the new types of tools that are being purchased and implemented, with virtually no input from the very people who are asked to use them. To make matters worse, the training plan for those staff members rarely exists, and many do not stay on the job long enough to gain the necessary knowledge. Over the last two years, I have had three to four office staff members leave their positions, and the new staff members who filled those vacancies received little to no formal training when taking over their tasks.

Will AI change that? I am not convinced that it will, due to the structural deficit that currently exists.

What Can Leaders Do?

Despite all that, I am looking forward to seeing how the advancement of AI will impact our support staff because their contribution is immeasurable. Just ask any classroom teacher how they feel about the support—or the lack of support—they receive from any of these staff members at school. Having a competent front office staff can make or break the whole school. When I was a young teacher, I knew a teacher who wanted to transfer to another school because the stress of not getting along with the copy clerk was getting to her.

As I was creating an outline for this book, I thought a lot about the time I spent working with our support staff members. I also thought about how much time my administrator colleagues spent considering the needs of our support staff. I am somewhat ashamed to admit that I haven't spent nearly as much time with them as I do with my teaching staff. In addition, I had to step back and consider what I could do for not just AI-enabled tools, but all technology tools.

The following recommendations apply to all technological advancements, including AI:

Recommendation 1: Establish a comprehensive inventory of all available tools

Before you get into anything else, you must know what tools are available to which staff member and how they are using the tools, with or without AI. This list should be updated regularly so that you can make informed decisions about future needs. This task shouldn't be offloaded to IT alone. I feel strongly that a school leader should know who is asked to use what technology tools so that we can champion a training schedule.

Recommendation 2: Establish a technology training program specifically designed for support staff

This will not happen unless someone champions it. Providing ongoing training for support staff will not only enhance the organization's productivity but also improve morale. A great administrative assistant can significantly enhance the quality of the school experience for many individuals within a school's ecosystem, and intentional investment in them is not a luxury, but a necessity.

Therefore, I suggest setting up monthly or quarterly training sessions on various technology tools that you know are being used at your site. This serves several purposes. First, you will quickly learn which tool is no longer being used by the staff. Second, the staff will be able to tell you what they would like to know in the future. Third, you will learn that the experts exist among them[43].

When I say, "experts among them," I am not just talking about technology skills. I am referring to a context-specific technology expert. How our textbook clerk uses Google Sheets may differ from how our counseling secretary uses it due to the nuances inherent in their respective roles. If you are fortunate enough to have several staff members with knowledge and expertise working in your organization, it's a good idea to encourage them to take turns teaching one another about the technology tools they use and know. This is particularly effective when the training session is constructed more as a brainstorming session. As they problem-solve and share tips and tricks on how to get things done

---

[43] I know a principal friend of mine who doesn't even have an assistant because the school is so small. In that case, you will probably need to rely on your county office, neighboring school district, or your parents.

easily and efficiently, they can also reveal the best solution for a specific pain point.

I am convinced that the important thing is to create a consistent structure to invite their contribution. By providing a structured time together, we can help build capacity among them. After hosting a few technology training sessions—which we can all do, if only to watch a YouTube video on how to use a tech tool together—I noticed that my office staff were consulting one another on how to use different tools more effectively without relying on formal training.

Recommendation 3: Solicit input from support staff who will be the users before purchasing a new tool

As important as providing training is, it is equally important to consider the support staff who will be using the tools at the front end, when purchasing new tools. One school district I worked for established a technology committee and invited all site-based registrars to solicit their input before choosing a Student Information System (SIS). I recall my school's registrar expressing her frustration at how the district ultimately chose a platform that she didn't necessarily want. However, she was much more amenable to participating in the subsequent training sessions for the SIS that the district chose, because she understood that there was no perfect tool, and she already had some familiarity with it based on her initial interaction. Despite her initial displeasure, she ended up becoming the de facto trainer for the district for years to come for any new registrar who was hired after the implementation. Additionally, she could provide context when the new registrar complained about the lack of certain features in comparison to other SIS that we ultimately did not choose.

Even though it took more time to choose the SIS, I saw the benefits of the process firsthand when I became the Instructional Technology Coach. When the district failed to host many input sessions while adopting another tool, that decision caused an implementation delay due to staff resistance after the purchase was made. Such a truncated adoption process will ultimately cost more, both in terms of time and resources. Obviously, it's not possible to host multiple input sessions. However, I strongly encourage school leaders to solicit input whenever possible because it will save time and effort in the long run.

Recommendation 4: Seek opportunities to improve conditions for support staff by sharing your personal interest and knowledge widely

Last year, I learned a lot about how AI technology is being used for sports equipment because my athletic trainer requested to purchase a new type of football helmet. Because I was interested in learning more about how the technology is widely being used for sports, I was able to engage him in subsequent conversations that led to our district adopting various tools to improve the athletic performances of our student-athletes.

This occurred because I happened to mention to him and other staff members who were listening to our conversation in the hallway that I have an interest in AI. Not only did I mention the articles that I wrote and the conferences I attended, but I also openly invited anyone who is using AI-enabled tools to share their experiences and knowledge. I expressed my desire to learn from them, the users. That explicit invitation resulted in other staff members sharing what they know, as well as the frustration that they felt about the tools we currently used. Therefore, I recommend that school leaders invite the support staff into knowledge-sharing conversations whenever possible.

Recommendation 5: Insist on cross-training

In a school system, it's common that support staff members need to perform multiple tasks. Because many of their tasks are often specialized and repetitive, some support staff members can miss seeing how everyone's job fits with one another to enhance everyone's overall experiences. It is important that school leaders build a culture of cross-training. Building a common knowledge on what AI can do to improve the overall productivity of the organization can naturally provide such an opportunity.

Recommendation 6: Supervise the implementation closely

As the saying goes, what gets monitored gets done. Closely monitoring the implementation of tools is crucial, and AI can be a significant aid. Many AI tools can be used to crunch data and create charts that are actually based on concrete datasets. Since I introduced the tools, I have seen our support staff use Gemini—we are a Google Workplace School, but it could be Microsoft Copilot or even ChatGPT—to quickly crunch data. They also love using Canva to create fliers or presentations. However, some staff members will revert to doing things they have always done unless someone is actively monitoring the implementation.

Checklist for Leaders

- Conduct a task and tool inventory to learn what your support staff actually uses, not just what's available
- Create and schedule role-specific tech trainings by hosting micro-PD aligned to actual tasks
- Prioritize cross-training to increase continuity and collaboration
- Regularly share updates on AI-enabled tools relevant to operational roles
- Solicit input before implementation by asking those who will use the tools what they need
- Monitor and evaluate usage data to identify training needs or inefficiencies

- Facilitate an annual tech audit and reflection session to surface hidden challenges
- Celebrate and elevate the contributions of support staff in tech and AI innovation stories whenever possible

Ready to Lead Wrap Up

The work of running a school cannot, and should not, rest solely on the shoulders of instructional staff. From the registrar managing transcripts to the security guard ensuring student safety to the cafeteria workers serving food to the students, every member of the support team plays a role in shaping the school experience. Unfortunately, they are often forgotten in the AI conversation. If we want AI to truly enhance education, however, we must expand our definition of who deserves investment, training, and trust.

School leaders should not treat support staff as afterthoughts, but as essential partners in innovation. By listening to their expertise, equipping them with tools and training, and creating systems that recognize their needs, we can unlock an often-overlooked source of creativity, efficiency, and school pride. Support staff members provide an enormous value to school life, and they deserve support from their leaders.

In the next chapter, we'll shift our focus to the students, the very reason schools exist. We'll explore how to ensure they are not only protected in an AI-powered world, but also prepared to engage with these tools ethically, critically, and creatively. From fostering youth agency to educating them on algorithmic harm, we'll examine what it takes to help students thrive as learners and well-informed citizens in the age of AI.

~

CHAPTER 5

Working with Students: Youth Voice and Agency

"You can't just give someone a creativity injection.
You have to create an environment for curiosity and a way
to encourage people and get the best out of them."
–Sir Ken Robinson, British author and speaker

Story from the Field: Student Agency and Student Leadership Development

As an immigrant working on learning to speak English, I realized early in my career that the best way for someone to learn something is to teach it to someone else. Although I was able to speak English well enough to earn my teaching credential, I learned more about how to communicate in English after I began teaching. It's the act of getting clear on how to communicate what you know that sharpened my knowledge of the English language.

As such, I have worked extremely hard to provide such opportunities for students whenever possible. This is one of the toughest things for a teacher to get used to because many of us are concerned that our students might not get enough content if we don't share what we know. This, more than any other reason, is why I believe many teachers continue to lecture to their students even though we know "*sit and get*[44]" is not the most impactful learning strategy. We erroneously believe that the students will learn from us if we can only tell them in a way that they can hear. However, I learned a long time ago that the more I allow my students to teach others, the better they learn the content. Because I considered myself as a learning-experience designer, not just a content-deliverer, I was able to focus on working to create conditions where my students could take charge of their own learning.

Below are a few examples of how I learned to gradually release responsibility to my students, and how that experience has helped me to create opportunities with AI.

Expository Reading and Writing Curriculum[45] Unit Creation Lesson

The first time I attempted to provide students agency for their own learning was when I taught senior English in Bakersfield. At the time, my district was implementing the Expository Reading and Writing Curriculum (ERWC) in junior and senior English classes. During the training sessions on how to teach the ERWC modules, I was also encouraged to write the modules as a teacher to teach.

I realized that the act of selecting high-quality nonfiction articles and then creating the modules that included pre-reading, reading, re-reading, pre-writing, writing, and re-writing was what made the ERWC module most impactful, in addition to what each unit was intended to achieve, which was teaching students to read and write nonfiction effectively.

---

[44] This is a term that educators use when we are attending a lecture or listening to a presentation to learn something.

[45] For more information, please visit https://writing.csusuccessCurriculum. org/.

After using the required curriculum with my students, I put my seniors in groups of four to have them create their own modules and teach them to the rest of the class. In addition to receiving two to three well-constructed modules, this process also allowed students to recognize the challenges of teaching a group of unfocused seniors. I also noticed that students were quite harsh towards their classmates when evaluating each other's work. Some students also emulated certain teacher behaviors, such as being strict about assignment deadlines or chastising their classmates for not paying attention during the lecture. When I conducted an evaluation of the process, several students criticized me for not doing my job of teaching them because I wasn't making every instructional decision.

Undoubtedly, it was a messy process. Still, I saw lots of positive growth among my students. In particular, they became very adept at choosing high-interest articles. I also learned about what my students cared about, such as video gaming, car racing, or even becoming a rancher or a jockey, because of the articles that they chose. Most importantly, I learned the importance of student agency and choice as the foundation for creating an authentic learning environment for all students.

Advising the Coding Club and the League of Legends Club

My desire for student-initiated activities that allow them to put themselves in the driver's seat continued when I volunteered to create and teach a Web Design Class despite not having a ton of coding experience myself. I knew that I could succeed by putting the right tools in front of my students to help them learn to code. My students used free tools such as Codeacademy to learn to code. I also wrote grants to gain access to free subscriptions to education tools such as CodeHS and Scratch.

Following my students' interest, I volunteered to be the advisor for the League of Legends[46] Club in 2012, supervising students who wanted to watch the gameplay on Twitch on YouTube during lunch. Because my students were so interested, the club took a field trip to Riot Games[47] headquarters to watch these gamers play live. The whole experience taught me to consider various matrices of success among my students.

For example, I had a student who was completely uninterested in doing anything in my English class. In fact, he barely got a D because he did the bare minimum. But he would show up on Saturday to spend hours working on *Lego Mindstorm* robots and was the first to sign up for the *Riot* field trip. He eventually went to a community college to receive an Information Technology (IT) certificate because he was interested in tinkering with computers and IT.

When I met him initially, he was a sophomore not on track to graduate. After I realized that he was failing most of his classes, I told him that he had to at least pass all his classes to graduate if he wanted to continue coming to my classroom during lunch to watch Twitch TV, which he had been doing.

Did I work to support him to be able to attend a university to pursue a degree in computer science? Absolutely! Was I successful in my original goal? Clearly not. But I still count him as a success since he was able to stay engaged in school long enough to find what he was interested in pursuing.

---

[46] A popular online multiple player game that has a world-wide audience. There are professional teams that compete, and it is one of the most commonly played games for electronic sports or esports.

[47] A company that created many popular online games including League of Legends.

Getting Out of Their Way

After moving to Mountain View High School, I started two student groups because I wanted to have direct access to students. The first group is the Principal's Advisory Council (PAC).

During the first year, I managed the interactions with a group of twenty-five students each month. For the second year, I asked a group of volunteers to lead the group, driving the agenda and creating activities. I met with these students once a month to hear about the pressing issues they wanted the administration to address. I continued to hear from our Associated Student Body student leaders, who were elected by their fellow students. However, the PAC students provided a triangulation point, allowing me to hear directly from yet another group of student leaders. Among other insights gleaned, I heard from them regarding how busy the lunch line was and how inconsistent grading practices were impacting students' mental health.

Creation of the Mountain View Principal's Technology Internship Program

The second student group I helped create was the MVHS Principal's Tech Internship Group. The group began as a way to offer more dual enrollment credits to help our students and to allow students with transportation challenges to have access to on-campus internship opportunities. It also served as a vehicle for me to gain access to the rich technical resources available among our students.

Developing Student Leaders as National Tech Leaders

As much as I adore my PAC members, I have done more work with the Tech Internship students. What started as a group of students who wanted to earn community college credits by participating in the on-campus internship program, the MVHS Principal's Tech Internship transformed into a group that speaks on AI nationally.

In November 2024, I invited Tiffany Taylor, then Vice President of the ASU+GSV Summit[48], to meet with our students. The students created a "pitch deck" to share what they wanted to accomplish, including providing more robust technology support to our school community. She advised them to think beyond and begin using their voices to speak on the topics that interested them. The first opportunity came when I received an invitation from the California Department of Education (CDE) to host a webinar on AI. Instead of participating in the webinar on my own, I asked Katherine Goyette, current Computer Science Coordinator at the CDE, whether I could include my students. She graciously agreed to let them lead a two-part webinar on AI.

The two-part webinar series[49] had over 8000 views on *Facebook* and another couple of hundred views on *YouTube*. The students spoke about a few tools that they used and the ethical concerns they had about the GenAI use in schools.

Since then, our students have presented at the Common Sense Media Summit on Kids and Families[50], the ASU+GSV Summit, and several other local conferences. They also hosted an event at a local elementary school to celebrate National AI Literacy Day in March 2025.

---

[48] https://www.asugsvsummit.com/

[49] They were titled, "From A to GenZ: Students Discuss the Future of AI - Part 1 (CDE)" https://www.youtube.com/watch?v=ATnHvdxYvlk, and "From A to GenZ: Students Discuss the Future of AI - Part 2 (CDE)" https://www.youtube.com/watch?v=jR8YJd1UfFo

[50] https://www.commonsensemedia.org/press-releses/common-sense-summit-on-kids-and-families-brings-together-national-leaders-to-address-critical-issues

Guiding Students to Become Tech Creators

In addition, I worked with a group of students to create what we call the AI Policy Pathway[51], a tool that school leaders can use to create an editable AI policy. This Google Innovator project was born out of my frustration with not being able to help my fellow school leaders. My students and I create a tech platform allowing a school leader to answer a series of questions to get an editable policy that they can edit with others.

The platform acts as a thoughtful guide to allow the model to generate the final product that is research-based and relevant to avoid wasting a school leader's time in having to wonder whether the policy that they generated using a commercially available LLM, such as ChatGPT, Claude, or Gemini. I know this because one of my students tried that earlier in our project, only to realize how generic and impractical the final policy was, even after inputting a full-page-length prompt to ChatGPT.

What Can Leaders Do?

The truth of the matter is that a school leader can do a lot when it comes to student leadership development. Because you can start any program at your school without anyone's permission as long as it supports your students directly, it's almost the easiest and most impactful way to influence youth.

Recommendation 1: Start a student group yourself

Perhaps the best thing that I did as a principal was creating the Tech Internship Program at Mountain View High School. What started as a simple way to provide our students with internship hours turned into a model program that other schools are interested in replicating.

---

[51] https://google-innovator-project.vercel.app/policy-generator

Of course, I am a big advocate of starting the technology group since I love technology. But any school leader can elevate student voice by creating an affinity group. It need not be technology-focused. You don't have to be a techy to start a group. It's not about your technology skills level. It's about how you create a structure to bring out the best from your students, and I guarantee that you will find students who are eager to share what they know with you and with the rest of your school community. It is a matter of creating a structure to invite that. If you are interested in learning more about how we did it step-by-step, please contact me via kipglazer.com.

Recommendation 2: Let the students lead

I consider this to be one of the most essential ingredients for success. When I was a teacher, I worked very hard to become "invisible" and "irrelevant" in my own classroom by the end of each school year. When I say invisible and irrelevant, I don't mean that I ceded all control to my students. I mean that I worked to support my students to be able to own their own learning without constantly having to rely on me to give them the exact steps. I focused on setting up the structure and environment that I believed would yield the desired behaviors from my students, then worked very hard to remove myself from the structure as quickly as I could. I did so by focusing on creating structures.

For example, my classroom had lots of containers with covers. Each held tools like color pencils, scissors, rulers, glue sticks, and other supplies that students would need to create. At the start of the school year, my students practiced various procedures including passing papers or submitting homework into different baskets. My students knew what to do when they were tardy, wanted to go to the restroom, or needed to ask follow-up questions. We also practiced what to do in the event of an emergency. A designated group of students in each class turned off the light when we were ready to show a video, grabbed the signs during fire drills, or even updated the homework board each day. We spent time on structures at the outset so that I, as a teacher, only needed to jump in when the students were truly stuck.

When I began the Internship Program, I did something similar. I recruited two students who I thought could lead the program and asked them to lead various projects. We created a website using Google Sites and then utilized Google Classroom to house all items, with the leaders managing the small projects. Although we had many successes, I, along with all the students, learned a lot from how things unfolded. For our second year, we have six student leaders who are leading the group. They each have four to five students assigned so that each can lead a small team for the remainder of the school year.

Recommendation 3: Create opportunities for students to experience new types of success

Based on all objective measures and standards, the MVHS Tech Internship Program has been extremely *successful*. Three of the students and I presented at both the ASU+GSV AI Show and the ASU+GSV Summit, and they were extremely well received. Several students participated in hosting the National AI Literacy Workshop at a local elementary school, and others participated in the two-part CDE Webinar series. They hosted a workshop with community leaders and other educators. We also hosted the leaders of the California Mathematics, Science, and Computer Science Program.

Although I continue to encourage our students to participate in various conferences, we are focused on the process of creation and learning from such experiences. At every event we participate in and every presentation we lead, we spend time together as a group to plan every detail. We discuss how to dress, stand, and deliver a presentation. Students write thank-you notes to the organizers.

Rather than having the core group of students continue presenting, we work on creating systemic success for years to come. Rather than allowing a few students to monopolize the spotlight, we work on rising together.

When we experienced setbacks, such as the Digital Wellbeing Challenge being cancelled or our project not being selected for the ISTE+ASCD Tech Challenge, we discussed how all these little lessons added up to important life lessons about perseverance and humility.

Recommendation 4: Learn with and from the students

While I am the adult in the situation, I am also keenly aware that our students possess expertise that I haven't had the opportunity to acquire. For example, I had to defer to several students in the group who knew how to code for the Google Innovator Project that we were working on. A student who knew how to use *Adobe Photoshop* taught the rest of the group, including me, how to create graphics for the card games that we developed.

In addition, I have learned so much from my students in terms of how they are using various tools such as *ChatGPT, Gamma, Canva,* and even various formulas in *Google Sheets*. I have learned to use tools that I had never considered using because my students mentioned them to me. If you are interested in how to support teachers, this might be one of the best ways for you to learn what is actually happening in the classroom. Students will tell you when you are working on a project together, and when you tell them that you would like to learn *with* and *from* them. Frankly, many of my students have become wonderful teachers for me!

Recommendation 5: Set a goal for yourself and the students

In my twenty-year career as an educator, I have led and advised many student groups. The most successful ones all had something in common: a target to hit. When I was the advisor for the Health Occupation Students of America, the group became so much more focused when we were getting ready for the State Competition. When I was advising the League of Legends Club, we set the goal of watching the live competition at the Spring Tournament in Los Angeles, which motivated our students to attend the meeting and raise funds. Even though I didn't start out to do so, once the students in the Tech Internship Program realized they would be able to present at a conference, they began taking their responsibilities much more seriously.

If you are considering establishing a program such as the Tech Internship Program, I strongly suggest that you think about having an achievable goal. If attending a national conference is not something that you are interested in or able to do, I suggest setting goals that are more achievable, such as hosting a technology tutorial for staff or providing tech support for their fellow students. Whatever the goals are, you will see students working to meet them.

Checklist for Leaders

+ Start a student leadership group that reflects your school's culture, values, or innovation priorities
+ Build clear structures and systems that empower students to manage their own projects and small teams
+ Promote student accomplishments through newsletters, social media, and school events to elevate visibility and pride
+ Leverage student talents intentionally by identifying and inviting students to contribute their expertise across campus initiatives

- Set achievable, meaningful goals for student groups to build focus, commitment, and a sense of shared purpose
- Create leadership succession plans to ensure sustainability beyond one class, year, or group of students
- Learn with and from your students by inviting them to co-create, teach, and reflect alongside you

> At their best, students are not just the recipients of their education; they are the co-creators of it.

Ready to Lead Wrap Up

At their best, students are not just the recipients of their education; they are the co-creators of it. Unfortunately, they are often not given the chance to shine as co-creators, partially because we didn't have the means to truly reach each and every student in the past. Although many attempts have previously been made to create individualized and differentiated learning experiences, we may now be able to actually do so with GenAI. But that can only occur when school leaders commit to building structures that nurture student agency, leadership, and voice. If we do this right, the results will ripple far beyond a single classroom or campus. As we've seen with programs like the MVHS Tech Internship, when students are given the tools, trust, and a meaningful goal, they rise to the occasion and often exceed it. I have seen it repeatedly, as a club advisor, class advisor, academic coach, and even now as a school leader. It is not easy, but it can be done. And the reward that you will get from it is immeasurable: for yourself as a leader and for the students you are supporting.

Empowering students in the age of AI isn't just about preparing them for the workforce or future technologies; it's also about equipping them with the skills necessary for their continued success as adults. It's about affirming their place in the present, recognizing their insights, and honoring their capacity to lead now. As principals, we must ask ourselves. Are we building systems that merely serve students? No doubt, and that is definitely a practical goal worth achieving. But to build systems that let students lead? That is an even more desirable goal worth achieving.

In the next chapter, we'll turn our attention to the families who send these students to us each day. From addressing AI-related fears to building trust and transparency around new technologies, we'll explore how to partner with families in ways that affirm their essential role in shaping a future-ready school community.

CHAPTER 6

~

Working with Families: Transparency and Trust

"If you want to go fast, go alone. If you want to go far, go together."
—African proverb

Story from the Field: Aftermath of the Ransomware Attack

When I first arrived at Mountain View High School, I learned that the district suffered a ransomware attack in 2021 (Morgan, 2021). As a result, the district lost many, if not nearly all, important documents. As a result, I had to recreate many basic documents that I should have had access to as the principal since I arrived in 2023.

Learning about this was so shocking to me that I didn't know how to reconcile my positive perception of the district, located in the heart of Silicon Valley, with what had actually occurred. Having worked under an extraordinarily disciplined and strict IT department in Bakersfield as a technology coach, I knew that the Kern High School District not only had a remote backup, but it also had an old-fashioned tape backup that was transported off-site daily. I witnessed how vigilant the technicians were about data security on a daily basis. I heard our IT director speak about how proud he was of his team for fending off numerous cyberattack attempts against the district. Kern High School District also had in-house coders who could address some of the needs that arise from purchasing off-the-shelf software, and so did Santa Barbara Unified, which my current district doesn't have.

When I shared my surprise—and frankly, sincere concerns regarding my personal data—with my current IT Director, he assured me that he had been working on correcting the practices since his arrival in 2020. In fact, I have seen our current IT department making a concerted effort in cybersecurity, such as sending test emails to staff to ensure they learn not to open emails that should raise suspicion, and sending reminders about how to combat such attempts.

Inconsistent Practices Using General Tech Tools

It is absolutely true that many, if not the majority, of my current school families know technology well. Many of them are even tech inventors. However, that doesn't mean the district can fully embrace the available technologies in a way that makes sense for schools. School leaders know that many commercially available technology tools are ineffective in a school context without significant modifications. Implementing these tools also requires a coordinated vision and ongoing training. Without both, a district can end up in a situation where either we have no good tool or too many tools that do the same things.

In the 2024-25 school year, our district conducted a comprehensive technology tools audit. I believe many districts had to conduct a similar activity because the ESSR funds were being cut. As a result, many districts, including ours, had to decide which tool to keep and which tool to discontinue. Whether a tool is being discontinued due to a budget cut or because a student has left a school, such an action can cause a significant disruption to students and their families.

Unforeseen Challenges

Because many of our parents work in the technology sector, many of our students are well-equipped with excellent tech tools, which is why our school has a Bring Your Own Device (BYOD) policy for students. Although we have Chromebooks available on campus, many of our students prefer to use their own device that has a larger screen and more processing power.

But that could create unexpected challenges. For instance, in the Spring of 2025, we experienced issues with many students during the Digital Advanced Placement (AP) testing because many MacBook computers had a security setting that would interfere with the testing software required by the College Board even though the College Board did not share that information with us. Until we discovered the cause, several students were unable to save their work as they took their tests. To remedy this issue, we are likely to require students to check out a Chromebook to use for AP testing.

I share these stories to illustrate that every school community experiences challenges regardless of its location in terms of tech knowledge or the access level of the community.

Working with Families

Whether I was in Bakersfield, La Cañada, Santa Barbara, or even Mountain View, I would say that parents want similar things when it comes to technologies in school. As educators, we know that parents want the school to ensure that their students are using technologies to learn and be successful. They want what every parent wants for his or her child: a positive learning environment that leads to success in life.

But how and what they would like us to do to achieve that goal can vary.

For example, at Mountain View High School, a parent wanted to meet with me and gave me a copy of *The Anxious Generation* by Jonathan Haidt. He expressed his profound concerns regarding unregulated cellphone use at school. He even offered to help me advance the idea with the Board and offered to build a cellphone container so that students could be cellphone-free in class. He was highly concerned about the mental health of our students who appear addicted to their phones. We also had a parent insist that her child's pictures not be included in the yearbook, even in its paper form. When we had to explain to her that we couldn't necessarily regulate any videos or photos of a public event, such as the football game, she was not pleased with our answers. We have parents who are very concerned about the use of cameras on campus and the surveillance culture that we are creating. Simultaneously, I frequently receive video footage from a doorbell camera when someone wants to report our students engaging in activities that the neighbors find objectionable. Finally, I have had parents reach out and complain to me about their children not being featured in the video recording of the AP Scholar Slideshow, only to discover that they have put their children on the "No-Photo" list.

Strangely, I have not had any parents reach out to express concerns regarding AI in any significant manner. Had it not been for the interactions with the students in the MVHS Principal's Internship Program, I might have thought that our parents had no clue as to what is occurring in schools with AI.

Engaging the Parent Community

Even if parents are not asking for the school to do something about AI directly, I feel that it was my responsibility as a principal to engage the parent community in a proactive and productive manner. In fact, I consider proactive engagement to be critical in building trust among parents. There were two events Mountain View hosted that can serve as a model: the first being the AI Learning Playlab and the second being the AI and Parent Education Night.

AI Learning Playlab

Before I get to what the AI Learning Playlab was, I must describe what led to hosting that event. AI Learning Playlab would have never occurred without the cancellation of the Digital Well-Being Challenge. Out of the disappointment of one event being cancelled came an incredible opportunity for parent engagement.

In December of 2024, I received a solicitation from the U. S. Department of Education. The email asked for a student group to participate in the Digital Well-being Challenge (see the graphic above).

After reading the solicitation, I worked with the group of students who were helping me design the AI Policy Pathway to submit the application. I considered this to be a perfect opportunity to elevate the work we were doing. I am convinced that policy work is integral to developing students' well-being. I was also hoping to use the prize money to finalize the AI Policy Pathway so that it would be a fully functioning digital platform.

As expected, our students were thrilled for the opportunity to participate in the national competition. Although I had to submit the application as the advisor, I shared the questions with students and asked them to write their submissions based on the provided rubric. Providing meaningful experiences for students should always be valued above all else. Even if they were not selected for the competition, the experience of researching and writing the response was equally important. Below is the answer that one of our students wrote to one of the questions that we submitted:

Are you a student aged 13+ or an educator passionate about improving digital citizenship and well-being in your school community? This is your chance to make a difference!

The Digital Well-Being Challenge invites schools and students to tackle pressing topics like healthy social media use, digital citizenship education, and responsible technology policies. This exciting initiative is a collaborative effort between the U.S. Department of Education's Office of Educational Technology (OET) and the Substance Abuse and Mental Health Administration (SAMHSA) at the U.S. Department of Health and Human Services.

What's in it for you?

- ✦ Collaborate as a school or district team to develop actionable solutions for local digital well-being challenges.

- Attend an exclusive virtual summit in March-April 2025 to connect with specialists in social media and youth mental health, safety- and privacy-by-design, and responsible technology use.
- Work with expert mentors to refine and implement your project ideas.
- Get at least $1,000 in prize funding that can be used to support implementation of your team project.
- Contribute to a Digital Well-Being Toolkit for national impact.

Don't miss this opportunity to shape the future of digital well-being in education.

Apply by January 9!

Together, we can empower school communities
to thrive in the digital age.

Learn more and submit your application today!

APPLY NOW

Figure 8: Email solicitation received from the Office of Educational Technology

Q. Please describe the problem statement related to digital citizenship and well-being that your school- or district-based team would like to address in the next 6-12 months. *

Reminder: Review the rubric that will be used to evaluate Challenge submissions.

This year, we launched the Tech Internship Program to provide technology support for our school community. Through this initiative, we identified a significant gap in our school's digital landscape: the absence of a comprehensive, student-friendly artificial intelligence (AI) policy. As AI technologies like ChatGPT become increasingly prevalent in education, it is essential to establish clear guidelines to ensure ethical, fair, and safe use of these tools.

The lack of an AI policy has led to confusion among students and educators. For example, teachers often emphasize AI guidelines before assignments, and students express concerns about what constitutes appropriate use versus misconduct. Instances of students being "caught" using AI tools, without clear guidelines to frame those incidents, highlight the pressing need for a shared understanding of expectations. In an article in our school's newspaper, students and educators discussed both the benefits and challenges of integrating AI into classrooms, further underscoring the importance of clarity and consensus in this new domain (see: MVHS Oracle Article).

Our goal is to co-design an AI policy that is not only robust and forward-thinking but also easy to understand and apply. This policy will empower students to use AI responsibly while equipping teachers and administrators with clear guidelines for enforcement. By aligning this effort with our school's strategic goals of fostering digital citizenship and well-being, we aim to create a safer, fairer, and more informed school community.

We will leverage the resources and infrastructure provided by the Tech Internship Program to spearhead this effort. The $1,000 in funding will support materials, workshops, and outreach efforts to engage students, teachers, and administrators in the co-design process. The program's structure also provides a unique platform for collaboration, enabling us to create a policy that reflects the diverse needs and perspectives of our school community.

When we received the following acceptance email and additional instructions regarding permission slips for our students, our team was excited:

> **From:** ▮▮▮▮▮▮▮
> **Sent:** Saturday, January 18, 2025 9:42 PM
> **To:** ▮▮▮▮▮▮▮▮
> **Subject:** Congratulations - Digital Well-Being Challenge Next Steps
>
> Dear Kip,
> We are delighted to inform you that your team, the Mountain View Tech Interns, has been selected to participate in the Digital Well-Being Challenge!
> Your innovative proposal stood out among many strong applications, and we're excited to work with you on bringing your ideas to life.
> **Next Steps:**
> 1.   **Participation Form Completion by Friday, January 31st**
>   - Please distribute the Participation Form to each member of your core team. This is the team of school leaders, educators, and students that will be participating in the Co-Design Summit and other Digital Well-Being Challenge activities.
>   - Each team member 18+ and the parents or guardians of student team members under 18 will need to complete the form.
>   - The team's primary point of contact should collect all completed forms and **email them in an encrypted or password-protected format to** ▮▮▮▮▮▮ , sara.trettin@ed.gov, **by January 31st.**
>   - Suggestions for encrypting or password-protecting the forms will be sent early next week.
>   This is a crucial step that must be completed before we can proceed with the Challenge activities.
> 2.   **Pre-Orientation & Summit Date Selection**
>   Please select your preferred Pre-Orientation and Summit dates by submitting this form as soon as possible: https://forms.office.com/g/713mLBCkkT. One submission per team, please.

If you have any questions or concerns, please don't hesitate to reach out to ███████████████████████

Once again, congratulations! We look forward to supporting your team's journey in co-designing innovative solutions to promote digital well-being.

Thanks!

The Digital Well-Being Challenge Team

Related Offering from our Friends at the AAP Center of Excellence on Social Media and Youth Mental Health:

Save the Date!

Join the **Virtual Youth Forum: Beyond the Likes - Social Media, Mental Health & You,** hosted by the American Academy of Pediatrics (AAP) Center of Excellence on Social Media and Youth Mental Health. This two-day event, happening **March 1 and March 8 from 10:00 AM to 2:30 PM CST**, invites young people (ages 14-24) from diverse backgrounds to explore how social media impacts mental health through fun, meaningful conversations.

The forum features interactive sessions led by youth from the Center's Youth Advisory Panel, mental health experts, and social media leaders. You'll learn tips for managing your social media feeds, understand how it affects your mental health, and build confidence to have open discussions with peers, parents, and others in your community.

You will have the opportunity to:

+ Hear directly from social media researchers about the impacts of social media on mental health and be able to ask them questions.
+ Receive training in how to use your voice to make change.
+ Learn how to spot when a friend may be struggling (and what to do!)

Sign up here to receive updates, including the registration link!

**Figure 9: Email communication regarding acceptance
to the Digital Wellbeing Challenge**

We then received another email regarding the next step on how to gain access to the resource materials to get ready for the Challenge:

From: ▆▆▆▆▆▆▆▆
Sent: Tuesday, January 28, 2025 2:32 PM
To: ▆▆▆▆▆▆▆▆▆▆▆▆▆▆
Subject: RE: Congratulations - Digital Well-Being Challenge Next Steps

Hi Kip,
Thank you for completing the form sharing your preferred Pre-Orientation and Summit dates!

The next step is to send your team's completed Participation Consent forms to me ▆▆▆▆▆▆▆▆▆ by this Friday, January 31ˢᵗ. Because these forms include personally identifiable information (PII), they need to be either password protected or encrypted before being sent. If you have a process or program that you typically use to password protect or encrypt files or folders, please feel free to use what you are familiar with. For your reference, I have included instructions for encrypting zip files and password protecting PDFs using a few different tools below. Please let me know if you are having trouble finding a tool that will work for you and we can troubleshoot.

Password Protecting a PDF
- **Adobe Acrobat** - If you have Adobe Acrobat on your computer you can follow these instructions to either Password Protect or Encrypt the PDF - https://helpx.adobe.com/acrobat/using/securing-pdfs-passwords.html.
    - To Password Protect scroll down to the section that says, "One-click option to protect a PDF with a password."
    - To Encrypt, scroll down to the section that says, "Advanced Password Protection"

- **Online Adobe Password Protection Tool** - If you don't have Adobe Acrobat installed on your computer, Adobe has a free password protection tool - https://www.adobe.com/acrobat/online/password-protect-pdf.html.
- **Preview on Mac** – If you are using a Mac, you can use Preview to password protect a PDF - https://support.apple.com/guide/preview/password-protect-a-pdf-prvw587dd90f/mac

Encrypting a Zip File
- **WinZip** – If you have WinZip on your computer, you can follow these instructions to encrypt a zip file that contains the team's completed consent forms: https://kb.winzip.com/help/help_actions_encrypt.htm

Thanks!

Figure 10: Email communication regarding the next steps of the Digital Wellbeing Challenge

Unfortunately, our excitement quickly turned to disappointment when we received a notification that the challenge had been put on pause:

Following up - Digital Well-Being Challenge Next Steps

Hi Kip,

I wanted to follow-up with a few updates about the Digital Well-Being Challenge.

We have communicated to our new political leadership about the Digital Well-Being Challenge and are waiting on the greenlight to continue moving forward. This is pretty typical – at the start of any new administration, there is a bit of a "holding pattern" as new political appointees are onboarded and they assess the alignment of current projects with their new priorities. While we are hopeful that the Challenge will receive the greenlight to continue, I do want to acknowledge that there is a chance we do not get approval to continue with the project.

We appreciate the work teams have put in so far with preparing their applications, assembling their teams, and submitting their consent forms – but we do want to wait until we have the greenlight before we ask you all to commit time to the Orientation or Summit. Because of this, here are the adjustments we are making:

1. **Canceling Orientation** - At this time, we are going to cancel the synchronous orientation sessions being planned for 2/27 and 3/1.
2. **Asynchronous Orientation Materials** - We are tweaking the orientation workbook and activities so that teams, if they choose, can complete these activities on their own. This might look like a series of shorter check-ins with your Challenge Team to work through the activities we'd planned for the Orientation to help further refine your problem statement in preparation for the Summit. Just like the Orientation, this is voluntary, but encouraged. We will send the workbook to team leads by this Friday.

3. **Continue holding current Summit dates** - We plan to keep the current Summit dates (3/22 and 4/5) with the goal of getting a greenlight by **Wednesday, March 12th.** If we do not get a greenlight or a redlight by 3/12, we will postpone the Summits and work with teams to identify dates that might work.

Finally, I also wanted to share that we are waiting on confirmation that the funding we'd previously secured for the prize payments is still available. There is a chance that even with a greenlight to continue the Challenge, we may not receive the funding for the prize payments. I realize this may be a decision point for some teams on whether they will continue participating and wanted to share this information.

Despite the uncertainty, the Challenge Planning Team remains excited about the Digital Well-Being Challenge and committed to the project. We know that you all are excited, too, and appreciate your flexibility during this period.

Please don't hesitate to reach out with any questions.

Thanks,

Figure 11: Email communication regarding the possible cancellation of the Digital Wellbeing Challenge

After receiving the above notice, I reached out to the student group to ask whether they wanted to continue the work despite the possibility of not being able to continue with the competition. Despite the setback, students wanted to continue. I asked whether they wanted to host an event to celebrate the National AI Literacy Day instead, and the students agreed.

National AI Literacy Day

The first National AI Literacy Day was celebrated on April 19, 2024. According to a press release by InnovateEDU, "The EDSAFE AI Alliance in partnership with The AI Education Project, AI for Education, Common Sense Media, and The Tech Interactive is calling for a nationwide day of action, inviting students, parents, educators, and other community members to explore the fundamental question, 'What is AI?' on April 19, 2024" (National AI Literacy Day, n.d.).

In 2025, the National AI Literacy was celebrated on Friday, March 28th, and I thought the Digital Wellbeing Challenge group could host an event to improve AI literacy in our community. According to the National AI Literacy website, every community was encouraged to participate and learn about AI, and I thought our students could certainly rise to the occasion.

As we brainstormed ideas, the students came up with a plan to host an expert panel during the school day and a play lab in the evening at a local elementary school. After hearing what the students wanted to do, I reached out to the Los Altos School District (LASD), our partner district, to see if they would be willing to host our student leaders for a community outreach event. Even though it was not exactly what we were planning to do when we applied for the Digital Well-Being Challenge, I felt that our students hosting the event to improve AI Literacy among younger students and their parents was honoring the spirit of the Challenge.

When I reached out to LASD, their Coordinator of Curriculum and Instruction got back to me immediately. She had heard about the Tech Internship Program, and she was open to allowing the students to come to one of the sites to host an AI Learning Playlab.

Final Structure of the AI Learning Playlab

Initially, our students wanted to have four stations for all the students and parents in a single space because we anticipated that only a small group would be interested. We thought we might get 25-30 participants. When we sent out a form to publicize the event, we had over one hundred participants interested in attending the event.

Based on the interest, we decided to have students create two workshops to engage both students and their parents in separate classrooms because the elementary school didn't have a large enough room to house all the interested participants. Our students titled these workshops: "Do's and Don'ts of AI," and "The Art of AI," showcasing tools that encourage creativity among users while providing important safety guidelines. Our intent was to support parents in their efforts to support their children as they transitioned from middle school to high school.

AI Expert Panel

We also worked on assembling four different speakers who could speak about AI. Because we wanted to have diverse opinions from various perspectives, we invited a tech founder, a superintendent, a researcher, and our own district's Director of Technology to speak on the panel.

To promote the event, one of our students shared an AI fact of the day via our LinkedIn and Instagram pages, promoting the event held on our campus. We invited various classes to attend the event and hear answers from the experts.

Figure 12: AI Learning Playlab Poster

Official cancellation of the Digital Well-Being Challenge

While we were focused on hosting a successful National AI Literacy Day event, we received word that the Digital Well-Being Challenge had been officially cancelled on March 14th, 2025:

Figure 13: Notification Email of the official cancellation of the Digital Wellbeing Challenge

By this time, we learned that the U. S. Department of Education had released a large workforce, including the person who was leading the Digital Well-Being Challenge. As a result, our final notification came from Digital Promise, not from an @ed.gov email address.

Keeping Andragogy in Mind

On March 28th, 2025, our students arrived at Blach Intermediate School to host the first AI Learning Playlab. In preparing for the event, the students learn about andragogy. Andragogy is a learning science theory advocated by Knowles (1970) and eventually developed into six core assumptions including adult learners' need to know why before learning, need for independence, need for validation of their personal experiences, need to connect learning to their real-life situations, need to center such life experiences, and preference for internal rewards over simple external motivations (Knowles, Holton, and Swanson 2005,64–68). I encouraged them to keep these assumptions in mind prior to building the workshop experiences.

Our students responded to the request by creating a parent presentation centered on scenarios:

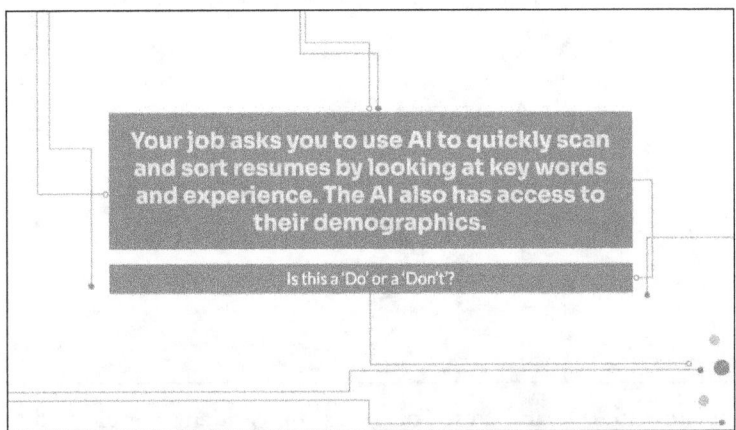

Figure 14: "Do and Don't" of AI Use for Parent Sample Slide

We knew that parents were more interested in learning about students' perspectives and experiences at high school so that they could help their own children when they entered high school, so we focused on delivering that content.

In the feedback survey, one parent said, "Loved the scenarios discussion and also the examples of what exact AI tools students are using…Thank you!" Another parent said, "The students were very knowledgeable and had copious insights to share both in their presentations and during the open-ended discussions. It's be [sic] interesting to hear from more teachers and parents who are builders of the technology." As I suspected, the parents responded to the workshop with support and kindness to our students who were brave enough to stand in front of a group of parents who work in the tech industry. In

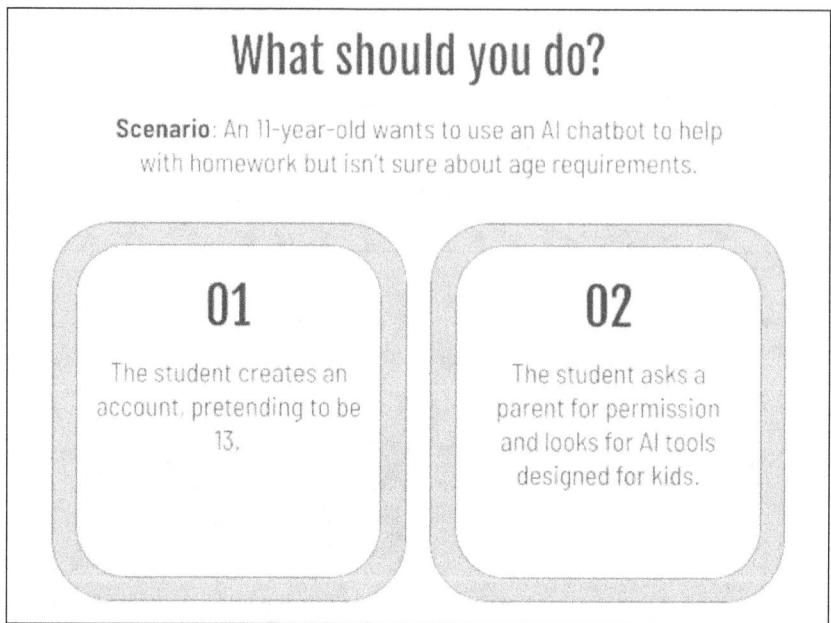

Figure 15: "Do and Don't" of AI Use for Student Sample Slide

fact, one of the parents was delighted to learn that our students were using *Gamma* because he worked for the company as a programmer.

This experience solidified our student leaders' understanding of providing what the community wants and has led to our next successful community activity.

Parent AI Information Night

In September 2025, our students hosted a parent evening. This was borne out of my desire to engage the parent community about the proliferation of AI tools.

I also received a few inquiries from parents who wanted me to ban cellphones at school. Our parents were clearly invested in having the school guide our students on AI, and I thought hosting an information night was a great way to engage the parent community.

Prior to hosting the event, I asked students in the Tech Internship Program to determine how they wanted to approach this. We arrived at the conclusion that we should survey parents to see what they might want from the school.

Surveying Parents, Staff, and Students

To begin, a small group of students created the survey. Since we wanted to follow up with parents later, we also requested their email addresses. We asked four questions listed below:

---

1. Your student's grade level. If more than one student, please check more than one grade.

- 9th
- 10th
- 11th
- 12th

2. What topics are you interested in being covered at the AI Info Night?*

- Preparing your student for future careers involving AI
- Helpful/safest AI tools that you and your student can use
- How AI is currently used by students and staff at MVHS
- Basic overview: what is AI and how does it work
- What jobs will AI potentially not replace in the future
- How to talk to your student about AI usage
- What does responsible use of AI look like
- Application of AI in the CTE Pathways offered at MVHS
- Open Q&A with the panel/admin/tech interns
- Other:

---

3. Who all would you like to hear from?*

+ Tech Interns
+ Administrators
+ Teachers
+ Other:

4. Anything else?

We deployed the survey over a two-week period and received sixty-three responses.

MVHS 2025 AI Parent Info Night Interest Form

Hosted by MVHS Tech Interns
Wednesday, September 24
6:30-7:45 p.m.
Location: SSB Dining Hall

On Wednesday, September 24, 2025, MVHS Tech Interns and administration will be hosting an AI Info Night dedicated to you as MVHS parents to learn more about what Artificial Intelligence (AI) is, how it's being used in education, its applications at MVHS, and what that means for your student and their future. We hope to provide a community conversation as to how MVHS can support our Spartans.

This event is designed to invite the parent community to share their perceptions. Our goal is for you to leave more informed and better prepared to help your student navigate a future where AI continues to become more integrated into the world of education and beyond.

To tailor this evening to your interests and concerns, please select the topics that you would want to learn more about. If there is something else that you would like to be discussed, feel free to write it below!

Figure 16: Screenshot of the parent survey

The parents primarily wanted to learn about how AI is currently used by students and staff (54/63), Helpful/safest AI tools that you and your student can use (39/63), Preparing your student for future careers involving AI (35/63), and What does responsible use of AI look like (35/63).

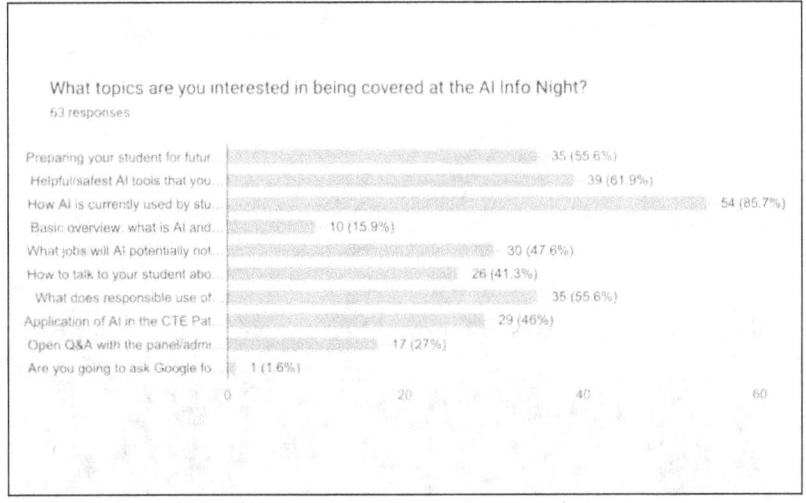

Figure 17: Parent Survey Response 1

They also wanted to hear from teachers the most:

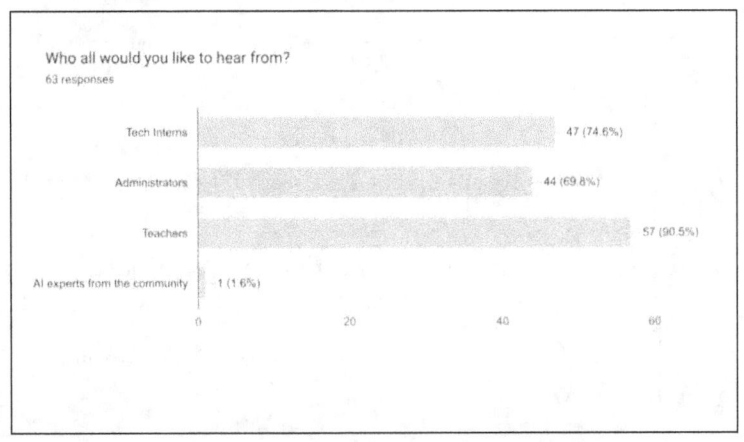

Figure 18: Parent Survey Response 2

Eventually, we decided to conduct additional surveys to gauge the thoughts of both students and staff regarding AI.

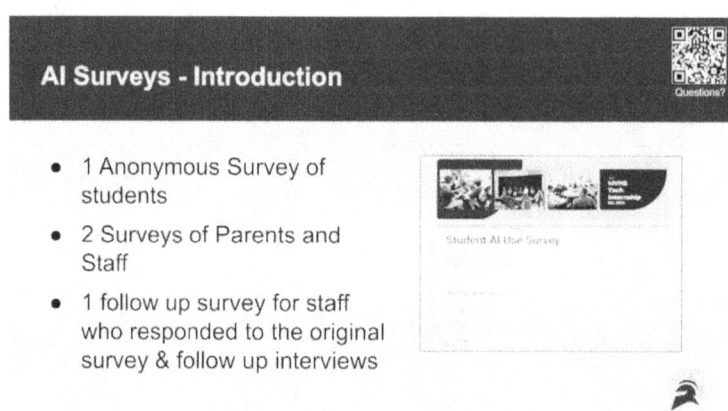

Figure 19: Survey Result for the AI Parent Night Screenshot 1

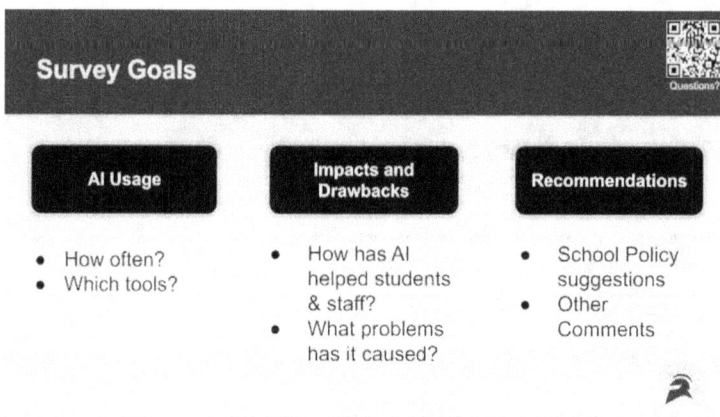

Figure 20: Survey Result for the AI Parent Night Screenshot 2

Based on our interns' recommendations, we distributed an anonymous student survey, which consisted of four parts: Student Grade, Student AI Usage, Current Effectiveness of AI, and What Can MVHS Do for You?

We had a total of 174 out of 2181 students answer, and the survey results were included in the final presentation that we shared during the event. Some key findings were:

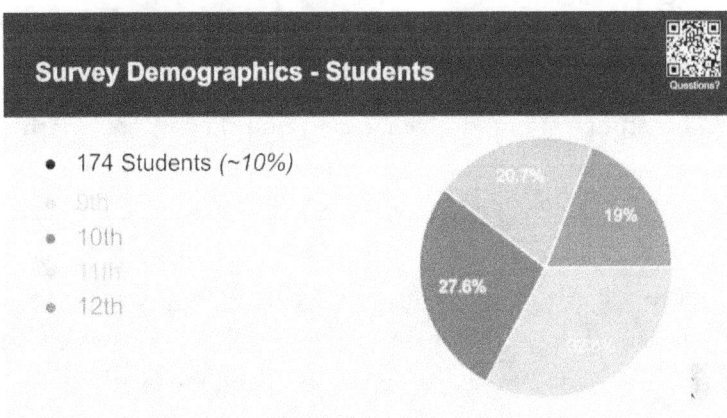

Figure 21: Survey Result for the AI Parent Night Screenshot 3

Finally, we sent out a staff survey. We received 63 responses out of 211 staff members. The initial survey that was sent to all staff consisted of three main sections: Essential Skills in the Age of AI, AI Use in the Classroom, and the Role of Parents.

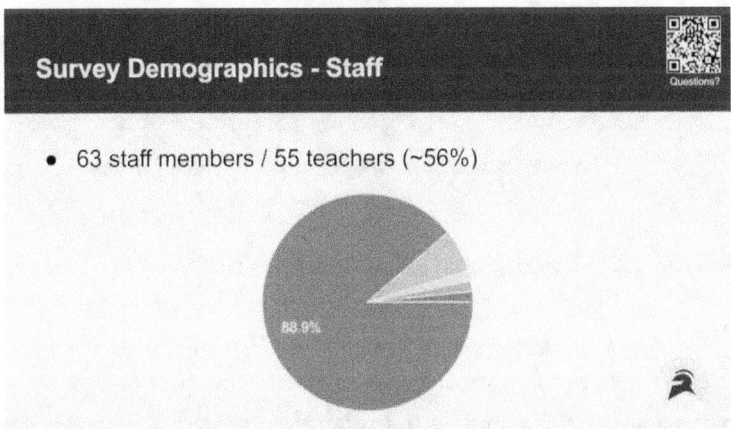

Figure 22: Survey Result for the AI Parent Night Screenshot 4

After seeing the results, we sent a follow-up survey to sixty-three staff members, asking about their use of AI.

Survey Results

Once we gathered the survey results, our students began analyzing and organizing them. Key takeaways from the surveys were that students use AI for studying and idea generation, and they wanted teachers to provide clear guidance on when and how to use AI for their learning. Staff reported that they frequently observe AI misuse and wanted the district and site administration to provide clear policy and guidance on students' use of AI in the classroom. Finally, parents wanted to know what was happening in the classroom and at school to provide support for their children and prepare them for the future with AI.

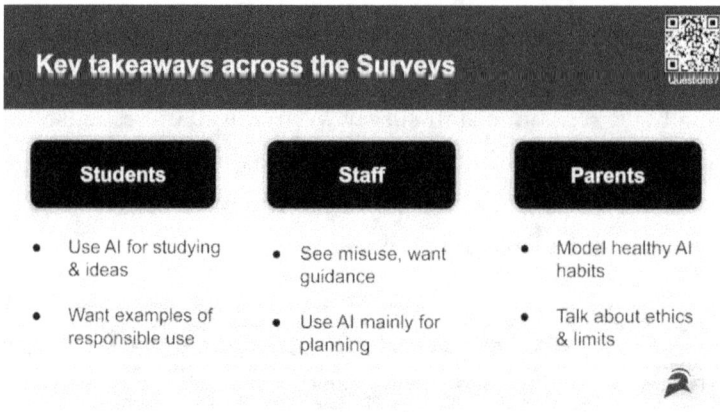

Figure 23: Survey Result for the AI Parent Night Screenshot 5

Hosting the Event and Future Plans

On Wednesday, September 24th, 2025, our students hosted the AI and Parent Education Event. We estimated that close to one hundred parents attended the event. Our students presented the survey results, posed questions to the panel members, and also answered questions from me regarding their participation in the Tech Internship Program and their interests as they gained more knowledge about AI by taking courses and working on projects such as the AI and Parent Education event.

Figure 24: Flyer for AI and Education Parent Night

When asked how they were using AI, students stated that they used it to generate ideas or fill the gap in their knowledge. One of the students who led the survey creation stated that he asked ChatGPT to review his questions to ensure they sounded neutral and bias-free before administering them to the target population. We learned a great deal from this experience, and we plan to host additional events in the future.

What Can Leaders Do?

With or without AI, parents would like schools to keep their children safe while setting their children up for future success. Because schools are still figuring things out when it comes to AI, building a strong partnership with parents has become so much more important.

Recommendation 1: Communicate, communicate, and communicate on all topics, not just on AI

If you are a parent, you know how many times you have to repeat yourself for your children to hear you, never mind listen to you. Or perhaps you have seen them use selective hearing skills. You probably did the same exact thing to your parents. If you are an educator, you know you have to repeat yourself many, many times for your students to learn, and the research is clear. Peterson & Peterson (1959) demonstrated that without rehearsal, information in short-term memory decays from 80% recall to less than 10% within just eighteen seconds, showing that repetition is essential for preventing rapid information loss and enabling consolidation into long-term memory.

As a school leader, I believe in over-communicating about important information. I have found that parents appreciate knowing what occurs at school. Although I didn't start it, I have kept up with sending a weekly newsletter called *Kip's Tips* that goes out to our community every Friday. I also post lots of happenings at school on Instagram to celebrate what is happening at school.

You might wonder if I use AI to create content. For my written communication, I have utilized tools such as Grammarly for grammar correction and NotebookLM to summarize lengthy content. I also use tools like Descript to edit my videos and add captions. However, I have written all my content myself so far. This doesn't mean that I have never used an AI tool. When I have used an AI tool to summarize any content, however, I communicate that upfront.

For example, recently I had to send a reminder to our school community with a lengthy document regarding the upcoming PSAT/ SAT test. So I put that document into NotebookLM to create a summary. In my message, I wrote the beginning part, and then I added a disclaimer before adding the summary.

Below is a summary of **this document** generated by NotebookLM.

Figure 25: Notification to the Community on my AI Use

Knowing that some may use an AI tool to summarize a lengthy document, I thought it was better for me to do the work so that we could minimize the impact on the environment as well as save time as a community. I also wanted our families, and students by extension, to learn how I am using AI.

After receiving my message, some students commented on seeing the disclaimer. Some stated that they didn't realize they could use AI to do what I did, while others commented that they were glad not to have to do the same exact thing that they would have done in the first place, since I already did the work. Being honest about how and what you use AI for is crucial in building and maintaining your professional trust.

Recommendation 2: Create opportunities for parent engagement

As you see in this chapter, it is vital for school leaders to create multiple opportunities for parent engagement, especially when it comes to AI. All school leaders should commit to creating ongoing dialogue on educational technologies including AI as we continue to experience its evolution.

Any educator will argue that positive reinforcement of skills acquired at school in homes yields better results. To guide such work so that the reinforcement is collaborative and productive, school leaders must model parental engagement.

Recommendation 3: Leverage the existing structure of engagement to connect with the families

Whatever we do, school leaders must think about the impact on families. With AI use, such responsibilities can be magnified and sometimes treacherous to manage. What helps me to ground myself in reality is remembering that schools have many existing structures of engagement. For example, many schools have a Back-to-School Night at the start of each school year. Many have a parent organization such as PTSA. Every school that I have been a part of has a system of communication to the families it serves.

Rather than trying to think of something brand new, I recommend that a school leader use what already exists within a school ecosystem to share what they already know about AI. A school website is an excellent platform to share what is happening at the school site, including AI. Using AI-enabled free tools such as Canva, a school can create simple flyers or even a newsletter to share the happenings. You can also add an agenda item regarding the school's AI use during a parent meeting.

Currently, my district doesn't have a specific AI policy, as our Acceptable Usage Policy encompasses all digital aspects. As peculiar and unusual as that may sound, relying on existing policies and procedures to create predictability can be an antidote to rapidly changing tools such as AI. As long as the existing structure and policy are family-friendly and student-centered, creating predictability can work wonders in supporting the families.

Recommendation 4: Solicit support from the community experts

Having worked in Bakersfield, La Cañada, Santa Barbara, and now Silicon Valley, I can say that every community has experts who are ready and willing to assist school leaders on various topics. When I was a teacher in Arvin, the Kiwanis Club members supported our students in attending a national competition. When I was at La Cañada, we had rocket scientists from the NASA Jet Propulsion Laboratory volunteering at our school. In Santa Barbara, we had many business leaders working with our students at the Entrepreneurship Academy. Recently, I had parents who work at Google reach out to me because they knew that I was working with our students on AI.

If you need experts in any area, including AI, there is someone in your community who can assist you, even if you are not in Silicon Valley. In each and every community, there are experts who would love to support their school leaders. You just have to ask for it.

I am not so naive to think that every community will have an AI expert. It won't. However, the point is to solicit whatever experts you have in your own community. The point is not to limit yourself in receiving support and to engage your parent community in a way that is expansive and positive by proactively engaging them.

Recommendation 5: Create a clear structure for effective parental engagement

However, it is critical that you are clear on what you want their help to look like. One thing I've learned over the years is that it's essential to be clear about your goals and establish boundaries upfront when seeking help from parents. Well-meaning parents who don't understand the school rules and systems can unintentionally add more burden than assistance. My recommendation is that you have a list of tasks that you want others to perform and seek explicit support for those tasks, not just on the topic of AI but in all aspects of school operations.

To achieve this, school leaders will need to invest time in determining the parameters and structure and have the courage to communicate them explicitly to achieve the best results. In fact, soliciting input regarding what the parameters or even structure should be can be a way to leverage community expertise. If you want them to give feedback or provide technical expertise, it is better to be upfront about what you need or don't need.

Over the years, I have had a group of parents who were experts in recruiting and training volunteers. Relying on their expertise has assisted me a great deal, as they can think of the benefits and challenges that I, a school leader, didn't consider, since that's not my typical area of expertise.

For example, we have a Pizza Cart that requires volunteers at our school on a daily basis. I have worked with the PTSA Volunteer Coordinator to use the ParentSquare Form, our official communication platform, to create a system. Rather than one of us coming up with a solution, I relied on parents' expertise to inform the creation of the structure. To get to where we are, I had to be clear about what we needed. For example, we needed a templated message, and we needed a schedule. As a result, the person who signs up to be a volunteer coordinator knows that one of their jobs is to send me a template message to be sent regularly to the larger school community. One of the parents created a video tutorial to train volunteers ahead of time to ease the onboarding process.

Setting up such systems may require some time, but it saves a great deal of headache and heartache down the road when everyone is clear about what the expectations are of one another. As Brené Brown (2018) said in her book *Dare to Lead*, "Clear is kind." Treating your parents with kindness by being explicit about your needs can pay off in the long run.

Recommendation 6: Share your own interest

Because I have been interested in the topic of AI, I have shared what I have learned with our parents. Writing articles and even writing this book is my way of letting the world, and our parents, know of my interest in AI in support of our students. Although no one can claim that they are experts in AI, I have not shied away from my interest in AI. I believe that such expression invites conversation from parents who want to make sure that their school leaders are able to stay current with various factors influencing education.

In today's school leadership environment, there is absolutely no way to avoid the impact of technology and AI. Even if you don't feel confident in your own knowledge, sharing what you know and what you are interested in with your families can help with your credibility as a leader who is interested in growth. Whatever way you can get the message out to your families, I would strongly recommend that you persist, so that they can be assured of your continued pursuit of excellence.

Checklist for Leaders

+ Model responsible AI use in all communications
+ Share lengthy documents with AI-generated summaries to save community time if you can

- Use AI tools transparently–Grammarly for grammar, NotebookLM for summaries–and share that with your community whenever you do
- Maintain authenticity by writing your own core content
- Schedule regular dialogues about educational technologies, either in a weekly newsletter or in various community meetings such as PTSA or Athletic Boosters meetings
- Host sessions specifically about AI in education
- Create ongoing (not one-time) engagement opportunities focused on positive technology use, including AI
- Use an already existing parent engagement structure, such as Back-to-School Night, to discuss AI and technology when you can
- Add AI topics to PTSA or other parent organization meeting agendas
- Update the school website with AI-related information
- Build on current communication systems rather than creating new ones
- Ensure all structures remain family-friendly and student-centered, regardless of whether AI is a part of it
- Identify AI and tech experts in your community and engage them
- Set explicit boundaries and parameters upfront
- Be specific about the help you're requesting
- Share what you're learning about AI with parents whenever you can to position yourself as a learner
- Express your interests openly, even if you are not an expert
- Demonstrate commitment to staying current with technology to ease anxiety among parents
- Use multiple channels so that there are more opportunities for parents to engage

Ready to Lead Wrap Up

If you ask today's school leaders, many will tell you that working with families can definitely be challenging. In fact, it's not uncommon for many educators to state that sometimes the adults cause more stress than the students they educate. Although that can be true in many situations, it is part of the responsibility of all school leaders to inform the community they serve.

A school is often the heart of the community that it serves, and as a school leader, a principal must care enough to understand and support the parents who send their most precious people in their lives to our schools. Whether it is about AI or other school-related items, I have always tried to think about what I wanted for our two boys as their mom. I wanted them to be safe and well-cared for while I wasn't with them. I wanted their teachers to treat them with respect and care, and I want them to learn to be good people who will gain skills to contribute when they graduate from high school and college. I believe that families I serve want the same things for their children. So I work to be transparent in how I am doing that with everything, including how I am managing AI in schools to the best of my abilities.

In the next chapter, we'll turn our attention to the world beyond schools that influence what happens in school. From the learning science research field to the education technology industry, there are many players that influence how AI-enabled tools are introduced to the school ecosystem. From writing articles to presenting at national and international conferences, we will explore how a school principal can influence the direction and focus of the AI conversation that significantly impacts schools.

CHAPTER 7

Working with the Research Field: Advocating for What Schools Truly Need

"What you do makes a difference, and you have to decide what kind of difference you want to make."
—Jane Goodall, English primatologist and anthropologist

Story from the Field: Expanding My Research Circles

In 2022, a dear colleague of mine, Dr. Pati Ruiz, who I met at Pepperdine, invited me to participate in a project funded by the US Department of Education. She asked me to participate in listening sessions hosted by Digital Promise. My participation in the listening session eventually led me to be a part of the launch of the Biden White House's seminal document, "Artificial Intelligence and the Future of Teaching and Learning," in 2023.

Although the YouTube video file of that webinar is no longer available, I was honored to be a part of the launch webinar moderated by Kristina Ishmael, then Deputy Director of the US Department of Education Office of Educational Technology. The panel included Jeremy Roschelle from Digital Promise, Jim Larimore from the EdSAFE AI Alliance, Tammy Lind from the South Milwaukee School District, and Thomas Phillip from the UC Berkeley School of Education. We discussed the potential and dangers of AI on teaching and learning.

Contributing as a Practitioner

My journey into learning more about AI began during my final year as a doctoral student at Pepperdine University. I took the opportunity to participate in a research project entitled the "Center for Innovative Research in Cyberlearning[52]," which eventually evolved into the "Center for Integrative Research in Computing and Learning Sciences (CIRCLS)[53]."

That's when I learned that there were grants funded by the National Science Foundation (NSF). Two professors, Dr. Eric Hamilton and Dr. Judi Fusco, at Pepperdine University were part of the community. While taking classes from them, I learned about what being a Primary Investigator (PI) on a grant project entailed.

I was fortunate that both of them provided me with incredible opportunities to participate in their grant projects. Dr. Hamilton allowed me to design a project that I wanted him to fund during summer break, which involved students guiding teachers in learning how to create digital games for their classrooms. Dr. Fusco encouraged me to share my perspective as a practitioner in the project that she was a part of.

---

[52] https://circlcenter.org/
[53] https://circls.org/

Even as a classroom teacher before starting my doctoral program, I volunteered to participate in research projects whenever I could. For example, I wrote a grant through Chico University in 2011 called "Teacher PD Inc.," where three teachers, including myself, received funds to participate in professional learning activities to improve our teaching practices. With the grant funding, I attended several conferences, including the *Learning and the Brain Conference*. This experience led me to create a YouTube video called "How Brain Learns" with my students and a teacher colleague of mine.

Figure 26: Screenshot of "How Brain Learns⁵⁴" (Glazer, 2011)

Once I began my program, I sought opportunities to join research projects in various capacities. For some projects, I served as a teacher participant, a proposal reviewer, or even a research subject. For others, I was an expert practitioner consultant. I initially volunteered for many of these projects for free because I felt that the learning I received was payment enough.

As I gained more experience, I began receiving a small honorarium or even hourly pay. I have also been invited to attend and present at a

---

⁵⁴ https://www.youtube.com/watch?v=szwbZQHwFRw

conference where a grant-funded project that I supported showcased its findings. I have also been asked to write a blog post, a testimonial, or a primer. Whether I am providing my expertise for free feedback or getting paid for it, each experience has been invaluable in helping me stay connected to the learning science field and gain additional knowledge on AI.

Because I stayed connected to the field even while I was working towards gaining more experience as a school administrator, I was given other opportunities that I didn't expect. I still remember speaking with Dr. Fusco one day when she asked if I knew anything about AI and was interested in any projects using AI. I jumped at the chance to learn more about AI because I had been thinking about the potential benefits of machine learning and adaptive assessment since taking the computer-adaptive Graduate Record Examinations (GRE).

As I was moving through the GRE exam, I thought about the way that the test was adapting to how accurate or inaccurate my answers were. I also wondered about the data being collected and how that might be used to design future assessments. This led me to reading more about AI and other types of adaptive technologies, including different assistive technology tools and data analytics software.

Working with Learning Science Researchers

I know that I am incredibly lucky to have had numerous opportunities to work with world-class researchers over the past decade. At one of the gatherings, I was so excited to meet Cindy Hmelo-Silver, one of the leading experts on problem-based learning and collaborative learning. I also had an opportunity to work with Jeremy Rochelle, one of the most cited authors in the field of learning sciences and technology in education.

Since 2014, I have continued to write and provide feedback on various NSF-funded projects. I have hosted multiple webinars for

Educator CIRCLS and have served as a member of the Practitioner Advisory Board for EngageAI since 2022. During one of the EngageAI convenings, I met several educators who were part of the Computer Science Teachers' Association (CSTA) and encouraged me to apply for the CSTA Equity Fellowship, now known as the CSTA Impact Fellowship. In 2023, I became a CSTA Equity fellow and co-created the "Framework for Administrators and Decision-makers on AI Implementation in Schools" with Sofía De Jesús, who was the Associate Program Manager at the Carnegie Mellon University Computer Science Academy. I also became a Google Certified Innovator in 2024.

Through it all, I continued to read articles and write on topics that I thought were relevant and interesting. For example, I submitted an article to Edweek, titled "No, AI Detection Won't Solve Cheating" in 2024, in which I strongly advocated for student involvement in AI policy creation and why relying on AI detection tools was an unproductive option for educators. I also wrote an article entitled "Why Leadership Matters in the Age of AI" for *Hello World* magazine in September 2024[55] to emphasize the need for strong leadership in educational institutions to support the ethical and safe adoption of AI. Finally, I served as a guest editor for the October/November/December 2024 issue of the *Literacy Today* magazine and wrote an article entitled "Redefining Literacy - what it means to be a literate person in the AI-Powered world," where I argued,

> [a] literate person in this new AI-powered world can no longer simply know how to read, understand, and produce written texts. **A literate person must possess information on a variety of tools that enable the expansive notion of literacy.** In other words, they must know how to leverage their extended cognition, such as a smartphone or a computer, much more effectively...a literate person must understand how these tools are being built

---

[55] https://www.raspberrypi.org/hello-world/issues/25

and programmed beyond being a simpler user of a tool. Because these tools will continue to evolve, **a literate person must possess computational thinking skills and data science knowledge to keep up with the advancement of such tools.** Understanding the basic technology that allows the development of new types of literacy should become the norm for all literate people, not the exception, in how we think about the development of literacy skills in this AI-powered world (Glazer 2024).

In addition to AI-related articles, I have written more scholarly articles. In May 2025, I became a co-author of a primer entitled "Social Regulation of Learning[56]" published by Digital Promise, where we discuss the different ways that students engaged in regulating behaviors when participating in collaborative learning experiences in a classroom (Hampton, Glazer, Dragnić-Cindrić, & Fusco, 2025). Although the primer had more to do with collaborative learning than AI, I learned a great deal by reading journal articles, writing, and editing the primer. Working with researchers and writing about learning-science related topics certainly kept my research muscle sharp!

What Can Leaders Do?

Obviously, I am not alone in pursuing continuing education opportunities. Most principals pursue advanced degrees and other professional passions. I see them on social media, sharing their day-to-day activities that are making a difference in their school community. Mine happens to be technology and AI. Some of my colleagues love sports, and they have gone to pursue exactly that.

For example, Dave Grissom, a former MVHS Principal, is now the current Commissioner of the Central Coast Section (CCS) of the

---

[56] https://digitalpromise.dspacedirect.org/server/api/core/bitstreams/d137a754-35bf-4f98-8097-0e96b483770d/contenwereresubmitt

California Interscholastic Federation. I see how excited he is about supporting our student athletes in his new capacity, even though he is no longer a high school principal. I know that he was involved in the CCS when he was the Principal at MVHS, and volunteered to represent the section at the state level for years before changing the role.

As a leader of an educational institute, a principal is the lead learner, and it is crucial that we continue to engage in growth and learning.

Recommendation 1: Read and listen widely

Although you picked this up because you want to read what a current principal is doing, I wrote this to be a practical guide for leadership. After spending close to ten years as a school leader, I felt that I had plenty to say just with my anecdotes. Still, I continue to read more books on leadership, writing, and applied statistics to expand my repertoire. The difference between now and when I was a doctoral student is that now I can use an AI tool like NotebookLM to summarize several journal articles before spending time reading them. I still read them, but I find the summaries useful in sorting and choosing good articles.

I also listened to lots of Podcast episodes to get a feel for what I should include in this book. I was determined to write a book that I wanted to read, which meant that it should be useful and practical. One such find was an episode of "The Mel Robbins Podcast" featuring an interview with Todd Rose, co-founder and CEO of Populace, a Boston-based think tank. After listening to him speak, I read his book *Collective Illusions*. That may not sound like an AI book, but it certainly has a lot of information about the negative impact of AI algorithms and social media on American society. Other books that have influenced me include: *Nudge: The Final Edition* by Richard H. Thaler and, Cass R. Sunstein, *Talking to Strangers* by Malcolm Gladwell, *Empire of AI* by Karen Hao, *Co-Intelligence* by Ethan Mollick, and *Unmasking AI* by Joy

Buolamwini. These books informed my stance on AI and propelled my desire to write this book for school principals.

I would be remiss if I didn't mention *The Generative Age* by Alana Winnick and *Designing Schools* by Sabba Quidwai. I highly recommend their books if you are interested in understanding how to work with your staff and fellow leaders who are grappling with the impact of AI in schools.

I also subscribe to the Harvard Business Review magazine, where I find many interesting articles on technology and leadership. By reading these books, articles, and other research journals, I stay connected to the learning science field, where I am continuing to learn and grow as an educator and school leader.

Recommendation 2: You set the speed or the volume

Some projects can launch you into specific spaces quickly, while others may never pan out. For example, I am still surprised how quickly I was able to become a principal[57], while I have been trying to convince my fellow educators of the benefits of game-based learning since 2015.

Whether you think it was too fast or too slow for someone else, you, as a school leader, must set the space that works for you and your school. I have always believed in setting my own pace that works for me and my school, and I hope you will consider doing so when it comes to interacting with and implementing AI in your school. Chasing a new shiny object has never worked out for anyone in the history of technology adoption, and we all know that technology and AI are not the silver bullets to "fix" all that ails our noble profession

---

[57] I spent one year as a Dean of Students, a beginning administrator who managed nothing but school disciplines and safety, and two years as an assistant principal prior to becoming a high school principal.

Recommendation 3: Put yourself out there to make a difference

As you can tell, I have done many things over the years to stay engaged in the field. As many times as my articles got published, an equal number of them—if not more—were rejected. I kept sending my articles to different publications because I was passionate about topics ranging from game-based learning and AI to school leadership.

I still recall speaking with Lisa Bonos, a Washington Post reporter, about an article she was working on in 2023. Even though I spent nearly an hour on the phone with her, none of what I said ended up in her article at the time. Two years later, she was writing another article on popular AI-enabled tools and how schools see them. Once again, I was not able to help her, but I managed to convince her to join me and my students at an event we were hosting.

Eventually, she wrote an article[58] about her experiences with my students to describe how I worked with the students to help a local elementary school district create an AI Philosophy Statement (Bonos, 2025).

Recommendation 4: Lean into your area of expertise.

As I began engaging with the learning science field, I realized that many researchers didn't have a ton of opportunities to interact with school leaders, post-pandemic. As a result, they often had to rely on their past experiences of what schools are like or what the media portrays schools to be.

But the AI research field definitely needs our voice. No matter how good a tool is, it can't get into the hands of the student without knowledgeable and supportive leaders in schools, and no one can understand what it's like to run a school in today's world unless you are doing it.

---

[58] https://wapo.st/4mLGx3ml

So I encourage you to always be who you are and do what you believe to be best for the students and staff you serve. Show up and share what you are doing, even if you are not an "AI expert" because there is no one who can claim that title at this moment. As a school leader, you have expertise in running a school, and that should be your calling card.

Recommendation 5: And please say yes to research(ers)

When a researcher approaches you as a principal, it might be daunting and even annoying to work with them. However, we can't improve our own field without good research in collaboration with practitioners. No matter where I was working, and even when there was no research institute nearby, I sought opportunities to partner with researchers because I was working to get better at being an educator and a school leader. Moreover, it certainly helped me to be a better teacher with classroom strategies that I used while I was teaching.

Early in my career, I was fortunate to get a taste of how research could impact my teaching practice when I applied for the Teacher PD grant that I mentioned earlier in this chapter. I was introduced to a seminal book, *How People Learn: Brain, Mind, Experience, and School*[59], published by the National Academies Press, while searching for a book on brain-based learning. This book changed my entire teaching practice, which led me to pursue a doctorate in learning technologies.

Since reading that book, I have worked with the researchers whenever I could because I believe in supporting those who are developing tools and practices to help our students learn. Unfortunately, so many researchers are not able to work with public schools, so their research findings can sometimes be incomplete. This is a huge problem in that we need more research to improve our teaching practices in support of

---

[59] https://nap.nationalacademies.org/catalog/9853/how-people-learn-brain-mind-experience-and-school-expanded-edition

our students who will be bombarded by AI in our classrooms. When a school leader believes in the value of partnering with researchers, not only will your students benefit, but also the education field at large will. Your teachers will also benefit by learning how the research is being conducted and what data will be collected. I strongly believe that more school leaders should partner with researchers to collect and present accurate data on the impact of AI. However, you should also be discerning of which researchers you allow in and whether they have respect for your teachers.

In the spring of 2025, we hosted a few Stanford researchers who were conducting AI image-generation research in science classes at MVHS. Before the researchers were allowed into the classroom, we had to ensure that all participating researchers were fingerprinted and cleared to be on a high school campus and to work with our students. Once they were cleared to be on campus, lead teachers met with researchers to ask several questions about the scope of the research. Then the researchers met with participating teachers to set the parameters and the timeline that would work for the students. The teachers also worked on the language of the permission slip for parents and students, including the purpose of the study, which AI tool the students would be using to do what, and an explanation of what students could do if they chose to opt out of the study, in addition to the standard permission slips that the researchers required for their study. I also visited the classroom while the researchers were on campus to ensure that everything went according to our initial plan. We also had to work with our IT Department to ensure that infrastructure support, such as strong WiFi, was available during the classroom activity. Although there was a significant amount of work that had to be done by many on our campus, I know that our effort has contributed to the field of education and AI use in science classrooms.

Checklist for Leaders

- Consider staying connected to a broader field as a part of what you do
- Read books related to your field of interest; they don't have to be on AI
- Review journal articles relevant to your work and use AI tools, like NotebookLM, to summarize articles before deep reading
- Podcasts can give you additional insights that you didn't think about, and get great book recommendations
- Define your own timeline and benchmark for professional goals; you are only competing against yourself
- Value your years of experience and passion as unique insights
- Set a tempo that works for you and your school
- Share your unique perspective when you can
- Submit articles or start a blog to share your thoughts and expertise
- Continue to share your thoughts or resubmit previously written items when the time is better
- Use your practical experience as your calling card
- Continue sharing even if you're not an "expert" in emerging technologies
- Build connections with researchers, even if initial attempts don't succeed
- Welcome researchers who approach your school to collaborate in their research project
- Involve teachers in understanding research processes and allow them to participate and grow as professionals
- Participate in a research project

Ready to Lead Wrap Up

I believe working within the research field is one of the areas that many school leaders may not be familiar with or interested in pursuing. Having been a busy principal myself, I completely understand and respect the sentiment. After all, we are hired to run a school, not add to the field. Still, without our voices in the mix of research and policy, we can't influence the future that is being created by outsiders who don't understand the reality of what goes on in today's complex school system. How many times have you heard an educator or a school leader lament about the people who believe they know what it's like to work at a school because they attended high school when they were young? Now more than ever before, we need educators and school leaders to be involved in co-constructing the future of education.

Still, I understand not many school leaders have the time or wherewithal to do everything recommended above. I don't expect you to. Instead, just follow the advice of Theodore Roosevelt, famously quoted in his autobiography. I believe that if you:

> Now more than ever before, we need educators and school leaders to be involved in co-constructing the future of education.

"[d]o what you can, with what you have, where you are," (Roosevelt, 1913, p. 329) we can all contribute to the field that we care so much about.

The Crucible of Leadership: Staying Human in an AI Age

"We are more alike, my friends, than we are unalike."
–Maya Angelou, American poet and writer

Story from the Field: Visiting Shanghai as an American School Leader

In July 2024, I was incredibly fortunate to attend the International Seminar for School Principals in Shanghai, hosted by the UNESCO Teacher Education Center and sponsored by the Shanghai Municipality.

On the second day, I had the opportunity to visit Shanghai Luwan Senior High School in Huangpu District[60]. The school had various technology labs, and I was able to use the Virtual Reality goggles that students were programming and visit their Robotics lab. The school was very proud of its AI lab, which had 5G capabilities.

---

[60] https://www.hpe.cn/ywb/latestnews/679243.htm

**Figure 27: Photo of 2024 International Seminar
for School Principals Table Sign**

I also met several student tour guides. When I asked one of them about their computer science curriculum, the student shared that they learned English by watching all the Harry Potter movies. When I asked them whether they knew how to code in Python, they all said yes. When I asked if they were a part of a special pathway to learn to code, the students seemed confused. Having gone through the Korean education system, which is similar to the Chinese education system, I knew what they would say. They confirmed that every student must learn Python in English to graduate from high school.

According to the National Center for Educational Statistics[61], there are 15.5 million high school students in the United States in 2024 (NCES, 2024). According to the 2024 State of Computer Science Education report[62] published by Code.org, about 6.4% of U.S. high school students are taking a foundational computer science course (Code.org, 2024).

---

[61] https://nces.ed.gov/fastfacts/display.asp?id=372#PK12-enrollment
[62] https://code.org/assets/advocacy/stateofcs/2024_state_of_cs.pdf

Compared to that, there are 80.5 million high school students in China[63] (Statista, 2024). Considering there are three, not four years in Chinese high schools, the total number of "high school" students in China would reach nearly 100 million. Even if 50% of the current Chinese high school students can learn Python successfully, that would be forty million Chinese people who can code in Python, compared to about one million American high school students who can do the same. This is a sobering statistic. Based on that calculation, there could be nearly eighty Chinese high school graduates for every American high school graduate who can code in Python.

As an American educator looking at the Chinese school system, I couldn't help but wonder whether we are preparing our students well for the age of AI. This experience has motivated me to continue engaging in the AI conversation and eventually to write this book. To be prepared for a new world where knowing how to use AI effectively is a requirement, not a "nice-to-have," school leaders must become well-versed in how to lead with AI.

Permission to Succeed

When I was about five years old, living in South Korea, I received a book of flags as a gift. Looking at all the flags, I was shocked to learn that there were so many more countries than my birthplace, South Korea, where I lived at the time. When my father, whom I respected as the intellectual giant in my young mind, came home that evening, I ran up to him and asked him, "Dad, did you know that there were over 150 countries in the world?"

He answered nonchalantly, "Of course."

I asked, "Which one is the number one country?"

He said, "United States."

[63] https://www.statista.com/topics/2090/education-in-china/#:~:text=Number%20of%20high%20school%20students,schools%20in%20China%202013%2D2023

"What about South Korea? What number are we?" I asked.

He said with a sigh, "Probably near the bottom."

So I asked, "Why don't we move to the United States?"

He dared, "Little girl. Not everyone can just pick up and go to the U. S., but if you want to, you can when you grow up."

I am not sure if my father even remembers granting me the ultimate permission that faithful day. But I believed him and believed in the promise of his words. Because he said I could, I made it happen nearly two decades later. I have spoken about that pivotal moment many times over the years because it represents something that I firmly believe in as an educator and school leader. However casual his comment was, my father's belief in the possibility and my capability opened the door for me to dream beyond what I thought was possible. Because I believed I had the permission and encouragement of someone I respected, I never stopped myself from working towards my ultimate goal of becoming an American citizen.

In many ways, I believe that is what we must do. Believe in the possibility of educators and students to learn and grow in the ever-changing world of AI. As leaders, we must give permission not only to ourselves, but also to the people we lead to explore, experiment, and engage with AI. Above all else, we need to tell them, "If you want to, you can."

Staying Human in the Age of AI

I believe the disruption that is being brought on by AI to the school ecosystem will feel like the most significant barrier to many educators. The unexpected nature of such challenges can certainly be overwhelming to many who didn't expect to encounter such disruption. Because the real impact of AI in schools remains both unknown and unknowable for now, educators and school leaders alike will likely struggle as we continue to navigate this uncertainty.

However, our charge to prepare our students to be ready for the world yet to be created, requires steady, inspirational—yet practical—school leadership, now more than ever before. Rather than fighting what isn't going well, today's leaders should strive to remain curious and ask better questions that lead to informed decisions, supporting the people they are leading. And we need to act now, doing what we can do and not focusing on what we cannot do.

> Because the real impact of AI in schools remains both unknown and unknowable for now, educators and school leaders alike will likely struggle as we continue to navigate this uncertainty.

In her annual letter[64], Amy Webb, CEO of Future Today Institute and one of my favorite thinkers, wrote:

> In an era of unrelenting change, **leaders must resist the temptation to wait for the dust to settle** and instead become astute observers of emerging signals, monitoring for subtle shifts in the competitive landscape that portend disruption. Quantum computing may not be accessible today, but actively engaging in "what if" scenarios thinking will challenge assumptions and prepare organizations for a range of potential futures, enhancing strategic resilience (Webb, 2024).

As Webb argued, today's leaders cannot simply wait for optimal conditions to occur. We must actively create such conditions for the people we lead by fully observing, monitoring, and engaging with AI.

To do that, a leader must be willing to make mistakes and iterate. As Alexander Pope said, "To err is human (Pope, 1711/1963, p. 159), and leaders must become fully human by trying things with and for the people that they lead.

---

[64] https://mailchi.mp/futuretodayinstitute/2024-annual-letter

In the AI Arena and Ready to Lead

I want to end with one of my favorite leadership quotes that I have been reading repeatedly as I navigate the challenging responsibilities and uncertainties that come with serving as a school leader. Theodore Roosevelt once said:

> It is not the critic who counts; not the man who points out how the strong man stumbles, or where the doer of deeds could have done them better. **The credit belongs to the [woman and] man who is actually in the arena,** whose face is marred by dust and sweat and blood; who strives valiantly; who errs, who comes short again and again, because there is no effort without error and shortcoming; but who does actually strive to do the deeds; who knows great enthusiasms, the great devotions; who spends [herself or] himself in a worthy cause; who at the best knows in the end the triumph of high achievement, and who at the worst, if [she or] he fails, at least fails while daring greatly, so that [her or] his place shall never be with those cold and timid souls who neither know victory nor defeat. (Roosevelt, 1910)

I know that being a school leader is incredibly tough, especially now amid geopolitical and technological uncertainties. We are all in this together, and I envision us continuing to lead, grow, and inspire. And being a leader definitely is more than a title. Every educator is a leader in his or her own right, and I appreciate you for embarking on a journey in leadership with me. From one leader to another, I thank you for being in the AI arena with me to pursue a noble goal of educating and supporting the future of this world so that we can make this world a better place together, and I sincerely hope that you are ready to lead with AI!

References

American Federation of Teachers. (2025, July 8). *AFT to launch National Academy for AI Instruction with Microsoft, OpenAI, Anthropic and United Federation of Teachers* [Press release]. https://www.aft.org/press-release/example-url

Clarke, A. C. (1973). Profiles of the future: *An inquiry into the limits of the possible* (Rev. ed.). Harper & Row.

BangBit Technologies. (2018, August 31). Introduction to artificial intelligence (AI): A deep dive into machine learning & deep learning. *Medium.* https://medium.com/@BangBitTech/introduction-to-artificial-intelligence-ai-a-deep-dive-into-machine-learning-deep-learning-4763e6985344

Berkovich, I. (2025). The rise of AI-assisted instructional leadership: Empirical survey of generative AI integration in school leadership and management work. *Frontiers in Education, 10, 1643023.* https://doi.org/10.3389/feduc.2025.1643023

Binkley, C. (2023, October 9). Schools' pandemic spending boosted tech companies. Did it help U.S. students? *AP News.* https://apnews.com/article/edtech-school-software-app-spending-pandemic-e2c803a30c5b6d34620956c228de7987

Blad, E. (2023, October 12). High absenteeism hits more schools, affecting students with strong attendance, too. *Education Week.* https://www.edweek.org/leadership/high-absenteeism-hits-more-schools-affecting-students-with-strong-attendance-too/2023/10

Bonos, L. (2025, October 5). This school district asked students to draft its AI policy. *The Washington Post.* https://wapo.st/4mLGx3l

Branch, G. F., Hanushek, E. A., & Rivkin, S. G. (2013). School leaders matter: Measuring the impact of effective principals. *Education Next*, *13(1)*, 62-69

Bransford, J. D., Brown, A. L., & Cocking, R. R. (Eds.). (2000). *How people learn: Brain, mind, experience, and school (Expanded ed.)*. National Academies Press. https://doi.org/10.17226/9853

Brockman, G. [@gdb]. (2025, January 12). o1 is a different kind of model. great performance requires using it in a new way relative to standard [Post]. X (formerly Twitter). https://x.com/gdb/status/1878489681702310392

Brown, B. (2018). *Dare to lead: Brave work. Tough conversations. Whole hearts.* Random House.

California Department of Education. (2024). DataQuest: Enrollment by school, 2023–24. Sacramento, CA: California Department of Education. https://dq.cde.ca.gov/dataquest/

California Department of Education. (2024). DataQuest: English learners enrolled and fluent English proficient students by district, 2023–24. Sacramento, CA: California Department of Education. https://dq.cde.ca.gov/dataquest/

California Department of Education. (2025, February 6). *From A to GenZ: Students Discuss the Future of AI - Part 1* (CDE) [Video]. YouTube. https://www.youtube.com/watch?v=ATnHvdxYvlk

California Department of Education. (2025, February 11). *From A to GenZ: Students Discuss the Future of AI - Part 2* (CDE) [Video]. YouTube. https://www.youtube.com/watch?v=jR8YJd1UfFo

California Department of Education. (2025, September 3). Learning with AI, learning about AI – Professional learning. https://www.cde.ca.gov/ci/pl/aiincalifornia.asp

Chambers, C. (2025, July 24). What a new survey says about teachers' plans to leave their jobs. *NEA Today*. https://www.nea.org/nea-today/all-news-articles/what-new-survey-says-about-teachers-plans-leave-their-jobs

Code.org, Computer Science Teachers Association, & Expanding Computing Education Pathways Alliance. (2024). *2024 State of computer science education.* https://code.org/assets/advocacy/stateofcs/2024_state_of_cs.pdf

REFERENCES

Cornell University. (n.d.). *Universal Design for Learning*. Retrieved from https://teaching.cornell.edu/universal-design-learning.

David Game College. (n.d.). GCSE AI Adaptive Learning Programme. https://www.davidgamecollege.com/courses/courses-overview/item/102/gcse-ai-adaptive-learning-programme

De Jesús, S., & Glazer, K. (2024). Framework for administrators and decision-makers on AI implementation in schools. https://docs.google.com/document/d/10x4uNpBsqPHyBo1FGLagC7j4P53Rjp4epkDbm1_sa3I/edit

Diliberti, M. K., Schwartz, H. L., Doan, S., Shapiro, A., Rainey, L. R., & Lake, R. J. (2024). Using artificial intelligence tools in K–12 classrooms (Research Report RRA956-21). RAND Corporation. https://www.rand.org/pubs/research_reports/RRA956-21.html

Doss, C. J., Bozick, R., Schwartz, H. L., Chu, L., Rainey, L. R., Woo, A., Reich, J., & Dukes, J. (2025). *AI use in schools is quickly increasing but guidance lags behind: Findings from the RAND survey panels* (Research Report No. RR-A4180-1). RAND Corporation. https://www.rand.org/pubs/research_reports/RRA4180-1.html

Hawke, E. (2015). *Rules for a knight*. Alfred A. Knopf.

GDPR.eu. (n.d.). What is GDPR? *The EU's new data protection law*. https://gdpr.eu/what-is-gdpr/

Glazer, K. (2011, December 14). *How brain learns* [Video]. *YouTube*. https://www.youtube.com/watch?v=szwbZQHwFRw

Glazer, K. (2024, April 12). No, AI detection won't solve cheating. *Education Week*. https://www.edweek.org/technology/opinion-no-ai-detection-wont-solve-cheating/2024/04 (edweek.org)

Glazer, K. (2024, October–December). *Redefining literacy – What it means to be a literate person in the AI-powered world*. Literacy Today, 40(2), 30–32. https://publuu.com/flip-book/24429/1497535

Glazer, K. (2024, September). Why leadership matters in the age of AI. *Hello World*, (25), 27-28. https://www.raspberrypi.org/hello-world/issues/25

Grandjean, M. (2015, October 14). GEPHI – Introduction to network analysis and visualization. http://www.martingrandjean.ch/gephi-introduction/

Grissom, J. A., Egalite, A. J., & Lindsay, C. A. (2021, February). How principals affect students and schools: A systematic synthesis of two decades of research (Report). The Wallace Foundation. https://doi.org/10.59656/EL-SB1065.001

Guerra-López, I. (2025, October 20). AI won't replace teachers—But teachers who use AI will change teaching. *Education Week*. https://www.edweek.org/technology/opinion-ai-wont-replace-teachers-but-teachers-who-use-ai-will-change-teaching/2025/10

Hampton, S., Glazer, K., Dragnić-Cindrić, D., & Fusco, J. (2025). *Social regulation of learning* [Primer]. Digital Promise. https://digitalpromise.dspacedirect.org/items/c522759d-e6a8-41f0-9e6d-c4881558f931

Horowitch, R. (2025, June 21). The computer-science bubble is bursting. *The Atlantic*. https://www.theatlantic.com/economy/archive/2025/06/computer-science-bubble-ai/683242/

Jetha, R., & Wallach, J. (2025, May 20). Silicon Valley's white-collar recession is hitting entry-level workers hardest. *The San Francisco Standard*. https://sfstandard.com/2025/05/20/silicon-valley-white-collar-recession-entry-level/

Kariuki, N. (2025). Economy. In N. Maslej et al., *Artificial intelligence index report 2025* (pp. 214–279). Stanford Institute for Human-Centered AI. https://hai.stanford.edu/assets/files/hai_ai-index-report-2025_chapter4_final.pdf

Keierleber, M. (2024, July 1). Whistleblower: L.A. schools' chatbot misused student data as tech co. crumbled. *The 74*. https://www.the74million.org/article/chatbot-los-angeles-whistleblower-allhere-ai/

Klein, A. (2020, January 7). What does big tech want from schools? (Spoiler alert: It's not money). *Education Week*. https://www.edweek.org/technology/what-does-big-tech-want-from-schools-spoiler-alert-its-not-money/2020/01

Knowles, M. S., Holton, E. F. III, & Swanson, R. A. (2020). *The adult learner: The definitive classic in adult education and human resource development* (9th ed.). Taylor & Francis. https://www.taylorfrancis.com/books/mono/10.4324/9780080481913/adult-learner-malcolm-knowles-elwood-holton-iii-richard-swanson

Kucirkova, N. (2024, May 13). Billions are spent on educational technology, but we don't know if it works. *The Conversation.* https://theconversation. com/billions-are-spent-on-educational-technology-but-we-dont-know-if-it-works-221280

Langreo, L. (2025, January 30). Schools' AI policies are still not clear to teachers and students. *Education Week.* https://www.edweek.org/technology/ schools-ai-policies-are-still-not-clear-to-teachers-and-students/2025/01

Leithwood, K., Harris, A., & Hopkins, D. (2020). Seven strong claims about successful school leadership (updated synthesis). *School Leadership & Management, 40(1),* 5–22.

Levi, S. D., Ridgway, W. E., Simon, D. A., Slawe, M. C., & Oh, A. (2024, April 5). Utah becomes first state to enact AI-centric consumer protection law. Skadden, Arps, Slate, Meagher & Flom LLP. https://www.skadden. com/insights/publications/2024/04/utah-becomes-first-state

Love, A., & Lee, S. W. (2025). Walking the leadership tightrope: Principals' experience of work–life balance. *Education Sciences, 15(10),* 1366. https://doi.org/10.3390/educsci15101366

Martin Grandjean - Grandjean, Martin (2014). "La connaissance est un réseau". Les Cahiers du Numérique 10 (3): 37-54. DOI:10.3166/ LCN.10.3.37-54.

Mathis, J. (2025, June 13). College grads are seeking their first jobs. Is AI in the way? The Week. https://theweek.com/tech/college-grads-first-jobs-artificial-intelligence

Morgan, Z. (2020, January 22). MVLA suffers ransomware attack. *Los Altos Online.* https://www.losaltosonline.com/schools/mvla-suffers-ransomware-attack/article_d2d501d2-4f1e-57a7-bbab-cd03b6ec789d. html

National AI Literacy Day. (n.d.). *National AI Literacy Day: What is AI?* https://www.ailiteracyday.org/

National Center for Education Statistics. (2023). Common Core of Data (CCD): Public Elementary/Secondary School Universe Survey, 2021– 22. U.S. Department of Education. https://nces.ed.gov/ccd/schoolsearc

National Center for Education Statistics. (2024). *Fast Facts: PK–12 enrollment.* U.S. Department of Education. https://nces.ed.gov/fastfacts/display.

asp?id=372#PK12-enrollment

NAACP. (2024). Artificial intelligence in predictive policing: Issue brief. https://naacp.org/resources/artificial-intelligence-predictive-policing-issue-brief

National Conference of State Legislatures. (2024, January 12). Artificial intelligence 2023 legislation. https://www.ncsl.org/technology-and-communication/artificial-intelligence-2023-legislation

Orwell, G. (1949). *1984*. Secker & Warburg.

Peterson, L. R., & Peterson, M. J. (1959). Short-term retention of individual verbal items. *Journal of Experimental Psychology, 58*(3), 193-198. https://doi.org/10.1037/h0049234

Pope, A. (1963). The poems of Alexander Pope (J. Butt, Ed.). Yale University Press. (Original work published 1711)

Quidwai, S. (2024). *Designing Schools: How design thinking makes YOU irreplaceable in the age of AI*. TeacherGoals Publishing

RAND Corporation. (2022, June 15). Teacher and principal stress running at twice the rate of general working public, hindering pandemic recovery [Press release]. https://www.rand.org/news/press/2022/06/15.html

Roosevelt, T. (1910, April 23). *Citizenship in a Republic* [Speech]. The American Presidency Project.https://www.presidency.ucsb.edu/documents/address-the-sorbonne-paris-france-citizenship-republic.

Roosevelt, T. (1913). An autobiography. Macmillan.

Ruiz, P., & Fusco, J. (2024, March 31). Glossary of artificial intelligence terms for educators. *CIRCLS*. https://www.circls.org/educatorcircls/ai-glossary

Statista. (2024). *Education in China*. Retrieved November 2, 2025, from https://www.statista.com/topics/2090/education-in-china/

Tarnoff, B. (2016, July 15). How the internet was invented. *The Guardian*. https://www.theguardian.com/technology/2016/jul/15/how-the-internet-was-invented-1976-arpa-kahn-cerf?utm_source=chatgpt.com

Turing, A. M. (1950). Computing machinery and intelligence. *Mind, 59*(236), 433-460. https://courses.cs.umbc.edu/471/papers/turing.pdf

REFERENCES

U.S. Department of Education, Office of Educational Technology. (2023). Artificial intelligence and the future of teaching and learning: Insights and recommendations. https://www.ed.gov/sites/ed/files/documents/ai-report/ai-report.pdf

U.S. Department of Education. (2025, April 11). Title IX and sex discrimination. https://www.ed.gov/laws-and-policy/civil-rights-laws/title-ix-and-sex-discrimination

U.S. Department of Health & Human Services. (n.d.). HIPAA home. https://www.hhs.gov/hipaa/index.html

Webb, A. (2024). *2024 Annual Letter*. Future Today Institute. https://mailchi.mp/futuretodayinstitute/2024-annual-letter

Woo, A., & Steiner, E. D. (2022). The wellbeing of secondary school principals one year into the COVID-19 pandemic: Insights from the American educator panels (Research Report: RR-A827-6). *RAND Corporation*. https://www.rand.org/pubs/research_reports/RRA827-6.html

Figures

About the Author

Dr. Kip Glazer is an award-winning educator and nationally recognized school leader with several decades of experience in learning science, educational technology, and AI in schools. A former classroom teacher, district-level technology coach, and current principal of a high school in the heart of Silicon Valley, she brings many decades of experience in innovative teaching strategies, leading educational initiatives, and effective technology implementation.

Glazer is a sought-after keynote speaker, conference presenter, and professional learning facilitator. In 2023, she was part of the launch webinar for the Biden White House's seminal document, "Artificial

Intelligence and the Future of Teaching and Learning." She also spoke at the Washington Post Live's Global Women's Summit in November 2025.

Considered an expert in AI implementation in schools, she has served as a practitioner advisor for several National Science Foundation-funded projects to bring high-quality research findings into schools.

Glazer is passionate about supporting the next generation of educators and school leaders. She has written many articles on AI that have been featured in EdWeek, EdSurge, and other notable publications. She is a fierce advocate of student agency. Connect with Kip at: kipglazer.com

More from
ConnectEDD Publishing

Since 2015, ConnectEDD has worked to transform education by empowering educators to become better-equipped to teach, learn, and lead. What started as a small company designed to provide professional learning events for educators has grown to include a variety of services to help educators and administrators address essential challenges. ConnectEDD offers instructional and leadership coaching, professional development workshops focusing on a variety of educational topics, a roster of nationally recognized educator associates who possess hands-on knowledge and experience, educational conferences custom-designed to meet the specific needs of schools, districts, and state/national organizations, and ongoing, personalized support, both virtually and onsite. In 2020, ConnectEDD expanded to include publishing services designed to provide busy educators with books and resources consisting of practical information on a wide variety of teaching, learning, and leadership topics. Please visit us online at connecteddpublishing.com or contact us at: info@connecteddpublishing.com

Recent Publications:

Live Your Excellence: Action Guide by Jimmy Casas

Culturize: Action Guide by Jimmy Casas

Daily Inspiration for Educators: Positive Thoughts for Every Day of the Year by Jimmy Casas

Eyes on Culture: Multiply Excellence in Your School by Emily Paschall

Pause. Breathe. Flourish. Living Your Best Life as an Educator by William D. Parker

L.E.A.R.N.E.R. Finding the True, Good, and Beautiful in Education by Marita Diffenbaugh

Educator Reflection Tips Volume II: Refining Our Practice by Jami Fowler-White

Handle With Care: Managing Difficult Situations in Schools with Dignity and Respect by Jimmy Casas and Joy Kelly

Disruptive Thinking: Preparing Learners for Their Future by Eric Sheninger

Permission to be Great: Increasing Engagement in Your School by Dan Butler

Daily Inspiration for Educators: Positive Thoughts for Every Day of the Year,Volume II by Jimmy Casas

The 6 Literacy Levers: Creating a Community of Readers by Brad Gustafson

The Educator's ATLAS: Your Roadmap to Engagement by Weston Kieschnick

In This Season: Words for the Heart by Todd Nesloney, LaNesha Tabb, Tanner Olson, and Alice Lee

Leading with a Humble Heart: A 40-Day Devotional for Leaders by Zac Bauermaster

Recalibrate the Culture: Our Why…Our Work…Our Values by Jimmy Casas

Creating Curious Classrooms: The Beauty of Questions by Emma Chiappetta

Crafting the Culture: 45 Reflections on What Matters Most by Joe Sanfelippo and Jeffrey Zoul

Improving School Mental Health: The Thriving School Community Solution by Charle Peck and Dr. Cameron Caswell

Building Authenticity: A Blueprint for the Leader Inside You by Todd Nesloney and Tyler Cook

Connecting Through Conversation: A Playbook for Talking with Kids by Erika Bare and Tiffany Burns

The Dream Factory: Designing a Purposeful Life by Mark Trumbo

Stories Behind Stances: Creating Empathy Through Hearing "The Other Side" by Chris Singleton

Happy Eyes: Becoming All Things to All People by Ryan Tillman

The Generative Age: Artificial Intelligence and the Future of Education by Alana Winnick

Recalibrate the Culture: Action Guide by Jimmy Casas

Leading with PEOPLE: A Six Pillar Framework for Fruitful Leadership by Zac Bauermaster

A School Leader's Guide to Reclaiming Purpose by Frederick C. Buskey

Foundations of an Elite Culture: Building Success with High Standards and a Positive Environment by David Arencibia

Personalize: Meeting the Needs of All Learners by Eric Sheninger and Nicki Slaugh

The Five Principles of Educator Professionalism: Rebuilding Trust in Schools by Nason Lollar

Words on the Wall: Culturizing Your Classroom For Observable Impact by Jimmy Casas and Cale Birk

School of Engagement: 45 Activities to Ignite Student Learning by Jonathan Alsheimer

Intentional Instructional Moves: Strategic Steps to Accelerate Student Learning by Sherry St. Clair

Overcoming Education: Complex Challenges, Difficult People, and the Art of Making a Difference by Brad R. Gustafson

The Language of Behavior: A Framework to Elevate Student Success by Charle Peck and Joshua Stamper

Whose Permission Are You Waiting For? An Educator's Guide to Doing What You Love by William D. Parker

The Leader You're Not…And Why It's Just As Important As the Leader You Are by Scott Borba

The Growth-Minded Leader by Tyler Cook

Day by Day: 180 Days of Hope and Encouragement by Zac Bauermaster

Make Your Move: For Ambitious People Ready to Live Their Aspirations by Marlon Styles, Jr.

The Hidden Work: What Separates Top Performers From Underachievers by Weston Kieschnick

Lifted to Lead: How a Paraplegic Orphan Rose from the Streets of Saigon to Become an American Leader by Stefan Bean and Kathy Nash

Lead From Who You Are: Leadership Isn't about Position—It's about Identity By Joe Sanfelippo